Guilty or Innocent?

Protecting
Throug
Nursing
Documentation

PALS 8.0

Doccementati 6.3 6/16/2016
13305

mastering 6.3 11/7/2016
Lab 13305

Rosale Lobo
RN, MSN, CNS, LNCC

MRP # 11 4/2017

EEP 13251

PHC
**PUBLISHING
GROUP**

PESI®
HealthCare
A division of CMI Education Institute, Inc.
A Non-profit Organization

Eau Claire, Wisconsin
2012

Published by
PHC Publishing Group
PESI HealthCare
PO Box 900
Eau Claire, WI 54702-0900

Printed in the United States of America

ISBN: 978-1-937661-04-5

PESI HealthCare strives to obtain knowledgeable authors and faculty
for its publications and seminars. The clinical recommendations
contained herein are the result of extensive author research and
review. Obviously, any recommendations for patient care must be
held up against individual circumstances at hand. To the best of our
knowledge any recommendations included by the author or faculty
reflect currently accepted practice. However, these recommendations
cannot be considered universal and complete. The authors and pub-
lisher repudiate any responsibility for unfavorable effects that result
from information, recommendations, undetected omissions or errors.
Professionals using this publication should research other original
sources of authority as well.

For information on this and other
PESI HealthCare products
please call 800-843-7763 or
visit our website at www.pesihealthcare.com

Editor: Barb Caffrey

Dedication

To my husband, for his love, dedication, support and belief that I could complete this book as planned and for loving me unconditionally.

To my three sons, Brian, Joaquim and Roy for their goofy ways, which keep me young and energetic.

To my parents, who instilled my undying thirst for knowledge that will last a lifetime.

To Brigitte, Ilona, Lorie, Renee, and Rachel for supporting this effort just because you wanted to.

To all the nurses who have dedicated their professional lives to care for the infirm. This book is particularly dedicated to you.

I thank you all.

Table of Contents

Part 2: The Not-So-Serious Side

Part 3: The Legal Side That Is Serious

Part 4: The Helpful Resources Side - *Appendices*

Part 5: The Side That is Last, But Not Least

Letters of Inclusion

To: Clinical and Administrative Nurses

From: **Rene Cabral-Daniels, JD, MPH**
Assistant Professor, Eastern Virginia Medical School

This book is a resource for the American healthcare system. Our nation is a highly litigious one and healthcare providers have experienced the negative consequences that accompany that fact. The practice of defensive medicine is necessary for all types of providers. The book's exploration of the many ways provider documentation protects those who render care is certainly of interest to a range of providers. However, the book is written by a nurse exclusively for nurses. This important focus means it has particular relevance for the one profession that has the greatest responsibility for patient care documentation. Nurses in any clinical setting will benefit from its clear depiction of how clinical documentation, performed well, is an important tool for the individual nurse as well as for the nursing profession.

Our nation is experiencing a huge transformation in its healthcare system and while much of the public's focus has been on cost, any attempt to rein in those costs will certainly and directly impact the manner in which care is delivered. The paradigm-shift that is affecting health policy makers' consideration of payment methodologies will be inextricably tied to care delivery. Healthcare provider payment systems are currently based, in large part, on the services provided. As both public and private health policy makers begin to shift their attention to patient outcomes as determinative of provider payment, patient documentation becomes directly related to revenue generation. The ability of providers to accurately document clinical care will no longer be the exclusive interest of those concerned with clinical issues, but will include hospital administrators and others who are responsible for the financial health of an organization.

Rosale Lobo's ability to target patient care documentation issues of interest to nurses makes her book a delightful read. It is also recommended reading for health policy makers and others who are responsible for transforming the healthcare system so that they understand the many challenges that confront nurses in rendering care.

Rene Cabral-Daniels
JD, MPH

From: **Rachel Cartwright-Vanzant, MS, RN, LHRM, CNS, FNC, LNCC**

One of the most influential founders of the nursing profession was Florence Nightingale. This Englishwoman transformed hospitals from a place of death and dying to a sanctuary of hope and healing. In spite of her own ill health, she was committed to, and continued to care for, the injured soldiers and ailing people. She was one of the early care givers who first recognized that inferior medical care caused so many British soldiers to die unnecessarily. She established the Nightingale School for Nurses in London when she was only forty years of age. She continued to be instrumental in the training of nurses and improving care until her death at age ninety. We can also recognize that inferior medical care can and should be managed with intention. As the following quote exemplifies: "I attribute my success to this: I never gave or took an excuse," Florence Nightingale. We can learn a lot from the tenacity and commitment Florence Nightingale's life portrayed.

We have entered into a period of time in which healthcare is undergoing many changes and presenting many challenges to all healthcare providers. Nurses still represent the largest force among all the healthcare disciplines and can have the most impact on patient outcomes simply by knowing what to do, when to do it, and how to do what is required. The final and equally important factor is the documentation that we do when rendering care.

We live in a litigious society, and now more than ever, nurses are at risk for exposure to litigation simply because documentation in the medical records is often shallow and inadequate, thereby allowing an opportunity for the litigators to challenge the care as reflected in the medical records. Regardless of whether the entries in the medical record are handwritten or electronic, nurses have a duty to maintain a complete and accurate recording of all the care provided. You must take this very seriously, lest you find yourself in the courtroom attempting to defend your care that you cannot even remember.

This book is written by a nurse for nurses and will provide many real life examples that will guide you in developing your own style of documentation that will intentionally put into place actions that will decrease your exposure to litigation. Times are changing and so must we. As we gain knowledge and become more experienced, the accountability for our actions increases proportionally. Documentation of the care provided is the only way to stand firm under scrutiny by demonstrating the standard of care has been met without question.

Rachel Cartwright-Vanzant
MS, RN, LHRM, CNS, FNC, LNCC

Part 1:
The Serious Side

Chapter 1
Prime Time Nursing:
Strategies for a Litigious-Free Career

What actions are required for a nurse to blemish their nursing license? I ask this because it seems like no one else is asking this question. Yet it needs to be asked, because nursing malpractice lawsuits are on the rise.

Documentation is the way we describe and defend the care that we provide. This factor about nursing is not an option, yet our voices regarding documentation are muted by so many other factors. Time constraints and electronic medical records are just a couple of the elements that determine if we will survive as defendants.

Nurses make up more than half of the professional healthcare team. Considering that nurses are vital to the ever changing and controversial healthcare climate, why are so many nurses feeling under pressure? Why do we feel, as a professional group of people, squeezed by the powers that be?

From the bedside to the universities, nursing is falling short of its expectations. Many people do not recognize nursing as a respectable profession and, sometimes, nurses find themselves thinking that, too. But we need to support each other and the nursing process. As a nurse since the 1980s, I can attest to the many ins and outs of a career that can be so rewarding and yet so damaging to our feelings of self worth. From the patients, right through to the administrators, then on to the doctors, we are faced with challenges that only another nurse can understand.

Has the nature of the healthcare climate changed for nurses? Yes, it has; the expectations are higher. Nurses are overwhelmed by what we really do not understand as the larger picture. We are being sued in record numbers, are the targets of denials in healthcare reimbursement and feel the overwhelming need for all to succeed. With these fast-paced changes occurring, we are forced to change the approach we take to caring for patients and the documentation that accompanies it. Imagine how many others read the entries you create when documenting. This information is used to support your care, but it is also used to help determine if new standards of care need to be created. Can your entries collectively shape the nursing processes? I believe that when nurses accurately document with a focus on quality data, we are able to continue to develop an evidence-based practice.

Bedside nurses are at the end of the information highway. We are often left out of the very essence of decisions that directly affect our practice environment. But sometimes, we are the last to offer support or lend a helping hand to our own. With increased knowledge of the bigger picture and a depth of understanding for our real mission as nurses, we can empower ourselves and feel as if recovery is just moments away. Understanding the core of how we defend the care we deliver comes right down to our documentation practices, the expectations of our employers, and the expectations that our facilities suffer from their intermediaries.

It is not necessary to nurse with the notion that you are going to be a defendant in a lawsuit. However, many of us do. Whether you work directly with patients inside a facility while they are awake or under anesthesia, as a telephone triage nurse, as part of a flight crew, in homes, in prisons, or even in a school, this book is designed with you in mind. Whether you are a manager or a manager-in-training, this information will strengthen the skills necessary to function with confidence. You no longer need to feel as if your license is in jeopardy. Having fundamental information about the nursing process will demonstrate the simplicity of the progression.

There are simple tidbits of useful information that will allow you to become powerful in your career. *What* and *when* you document is crucial, but deciding *how* to do it takes inside knowledge that nursing school or orientation doesn't teach. It is shocking to realize that in all our training, we are never really given a full explanation of why we are making errors in our documentation.

Plaintiff lawyers take the information in the medical record, plus your testimony, and come up with a story that they hope a jury will believe—a story based on the patient's bad outcome and the information in the record. Crafting a story that demonstrates you cared for your patient according to all the guidelines requires some introspection. With a little investment of time on the front end, your nursing life can have less stress and perhaps more gratitude.

Remember that your documentation is judged by written standards that are publicly available from federal and state guidelines to professional associations and your facility's policies and procedures. These are the sources that will be used by medical malpractice attorneys. Once you spend some time reading this book and applying the information to your practice, documentation will be less of a mystery and more of a power tool towards your continued success as a nurse.

Chapter 2
The Role of the Legal Nurse Consultant

You get that dreaded call from the risk management department. You provided care to a patient who is now suing the facility. You will be required to meet with the risk management department to discuss the events in the case. They give you a brief overview of the case and ask you to begin thinking about the care you provided to the patient last year. But how can they expect you to remember specific events from the previous year? More often than not, nurses will not remember the patient at all.

Having a documentation system is the key to saving your license and reputation if there is a disgruntled patient. The allegations are bad, and may feel like a final ruling, but they are just the beginning of a long legal dilemma. Walking through the events that occur in the litigation process will allow you to see the ultimate purpose for a personal accountability system.

Before a nurse has the desire to embark on a project like this, you must examine why there is urgency. Your facility, which will be eager to impress upon you its bottom line, will not motivate an employee to document in a specific way unless the facility's bottom line, in turn, affects yours. (Why should you care if you are "nickel-and-diming" your job into the black?) The motivation needs to come from within. You need to realize how a system like this could have value to your livelihood.

Nursing is one of those professions that encompass many entities. If you are a clinical practitioner, a manager, or supervisor, the information regarding quality, compliance, workflow, regulations, policy, and outcomes often trickles down and loses impact. In most cases, it is believed that only the administrator of a facility has access to all the information regarding rules and regulations and the issues that require risk management interventions and/or the legal department. The administrators are privy to the federal and state regulatory changes required in documentation standards. But what most people don't realize is this: *you are, too*—because state and federal guidelines are open to the public. However, the healthcare administrators determine how their facilities will develop the language necessary to execute the requirements. Those are the policies and procedures of your workplace.

Once the administrator and senior staff members embark upon these changes, the information is distributed according to the chain of command. Eventually, you hear about it. Sometimes the information is fragmented with inferences and juxtaposition. Getting the final statement of change that is expected can be confusing.

As humans, we are more inclined to follow a directive if we can conceptualize the aftermath. For nurses, it is even more concrete. For example, when a patient presents with signs and symptoms of a cardiac event, we know from experience and education that immediate intervention will either save this person's life, prevent permanent damage, or simply take him away from his discomfort.

We are *tangible* professionals. Touching, hearing, feeling and seeing are all skills we use daily in order to get the job done. We might even carry this behavior over into our personal lives. Having proof helps us to understand. The adage "trust, but verify" can be quite valuable in many situations.

The urgency that you need in order to develop a system of documentation often comes from a clear mental picture of the "what ifs," but I would rather you experience a medical malpractice case though someone else's experience. The urgency factor should come from knowing that, without a system of checks and balances for yourself, there could be unanswered questions regarding the care you provided. That is far too painful of a lesson, because having to attend a deposition where the opposing attorney is asking how you upheld the standard of care for your facility is not a great place to be. Instead, I'd rather you experience the horror from my perspective.

Changes in healthcare are moving at record pace. Many nurses find themselves moving rapidly, too, but just because you're moving doesn't necessarily mean you are going anywhere. (Picture a person in a rocking chair.) In other words, our movements need to be purposeful to be effective.

A systemic approach to nursing is important. Being able to track your workflow, actions, reactions, and critical thinking takes some examination.

Why does a person who has a bad outcome end up filing a lawsuit? Because both the healthcare environment and the law tend to follow well-defined systems, and they expect nurses to do the same. Nurses—this is why we *must* follow a system.

A patient has a bad experience at a healthcare facility. He or she is upset about the way he or she feels or looks after being treated in a healthcare setting. For example, suppose someone was in a terrible accident and he suffered an injury to his leg. He sought medical care; ultimately, his leg is amputated. After this, he might seek the assistance of an attorney because he feels the healthcare providers may have amputated his leg without cause. This might sound ridiculous, but sometimes allegations are. The patient/client will explain his or her side of the story to the lawyer. The lawyer wants to believe his client.

But before the lawyer believes everything the client says, the lawyer in question will get permission from the patient to get a copy of his medical records from the healthcare facility. The lawyer might tell the client that although the allegation sounds horrible, we cannot be certain there is an actual case until the records are received and examined by someone who can speak to the care provided and assure us that what was done fell outside the standard of care.

Next, the client gives the attorney permission and the records are requested.

Once the records are received, they are organized. There are several ways law firms choose to categorize the records. Some use a system called *Bates stamping*. Once all the records have been organized according to department and date, they are stamped in numerical order. When multiple copies are made, everyone referring to a page in the record can refer to the page by its Bates-stamped number. A more common way would be to put them in the same order as the hospital's or clinic's chart. The goal is to place the information chronologically to demonstrate events as they happen. Regardless of the format in which the medical records are received, they are placed in organized binders or notebooks so the information can be studied.

The record is analyzed according to the assessments, interventions, and evaluations. This sounds simple. Well, it can be. But it gets complicated when there are many things happening at the same time and the simple things are missed.

The record is read like a non-fiction story with characters and situations that seems to come alive with detail. Sometimes, important information is missing, which makes the nurse look like he or she has been negligent. The documentation in the medical record is the evidence needed to begin the lawsuit. Other documents are used after the lawsuit is filed, but the lawyer needs only the documentation in question to begin the lawsuit process. If the chart is found to have evidence that deviates from the standard of care without further explanation, and a professional in the same specialty has confirmed this, a lawsuit will be filed.

There are many steps in a lawsuit. In many situations, the nurse will not be privy to them since the role of the plaintiff nurse consultant is the analysis of the documentation. There is a time when your sworn statement, or *deposition*, will be taken. During the deposition, the plaintiff's attorney is able to ask you questions about your education, professional career, how you perform certain skills in a clinical setting and most importantly about the entries you made in the record and what you can recall about the presentation of the case. Of all the questioning that occurs, there will be the ones on standard of care.

Suppose the case was about sedating someone who was combative. Care needs to be taken in the documentation of this event. There are regulations stating that medication is not to be given as a form of restraint. As a nurse, you know this. But the attorney questioning you is skilled at interrogation. This question, and others like it, could be asked repeatedly in a manner unbeknownst to you.

A deposition involves you being sworn in, with a court reporter noting everything you say. After the deposition, the plaintiff's attorney will get a copy and review the information that was gleaned from it. They are hoping to read information that will further incriminate you. Depositions can take many hours and are usually stressful.

Having a system to your workflow will minimize your risk of being in the hot defendant's seat. *That's why this book is designed with you in mind.*

The book's first part will outline the necessary steps needed for strategic planning. It is important as a nurse for you to have a plan within your nursing day. We manage too many interruptions and often times there are no checks and balances until someone brings it to our attention. Sometimes, that's too late.

Strategic planning is a habit employed by every business you can think of. It is the foundation of strategic planning that allows a business to survive and accomplish whatever it sets out to do. Nurses are similar to business owners, because it is our licenses that allow us to earn a living.

The second part of this book is comprised of fictional stories that involve nurses. They are fiction, but as a legal nurse consultant, I have come to realize that many times we are faced with inconvenient variables that disrupt our ability to provide care and use critical thinking skills while under time constraints. The stories included are designed to provoke thought about the situations with which you are faced regularly.

The third part of this book is about the serious side of documentation: the time when a patient has turned into a client. There are actual cases and deposition testimony that demonstrate that attorneys have done extensive research and preparation regarding the events that occurred that might have caused deviations in the standard of care. They are expert interrogators, and although the question and answer sessions are not meant to intimidate you, often times they will. Lawyers structure their questions on your experience, the documentation, the standard of practice and the patient's injuries. Attorneys derive their information from sources that are also available to you. Medicare and Medicaid have standards of practice. These can be found on their Web sites. Joint Commission has standards of practice and again these can be found on its website. Individual states have statutes and regulations that describe the way certain things in healthcare and other regulated businesses should be done. This information is open to the public and the law is clear on the way patients are to be managed. Lawyers use these sources everyday to prove their cases, which is why the documents that you create as a non-fiction storyteller must demonstrate that you are following these rules. There are so many times that nurses are following the rules, but the act of documenting the poignant events are accidentally omitted. A systemic approach to documentation is your personal accountability system; use a system to keep your license blemish-free. Part Three helps you understand that.

Part Four includes resources. Spending time outside of work developing a system of professional management is not a bad idea. Many nurses might think that the system they have in place works just fine. You might not need to read any further. If that is the case, please spend some time reading the cases and deposition testimony. The tone of questioning makes clear that without a systematic approach to nursing care, an attorney could question you on a situation that occurred many months or even years ago.

Chapter 3
Why Should I Bother to Develop a Strategy?

When you began your nursing career, you might have had a clear idea of what you would be doing. You knew that taking care of patients was your main concern. Clinical rotations and eventually, orientation and unit assignments, came and the role of nurse was upon you. With all the knowledge and tests to be had, it is still very difficult for nurses to negotiate their environments with the time constraints and assurance needed. Nurses learn enough to be safe practitioners and pass the state exams. Like most professions, the real knowledge and experience is gained once the person is earning a salary.

In all the training that we receive, little attention is paid to the logistics of getting the work done. Documenting the events in an organized system where the net result is a story of your ability to use good judgment. This outcome will not be questioned by the legal system. Nurses are being named in lawsuits more often these days, so learning a strategy to get through your shift is more important today than ten or even five years ago.

Having a system within your nursing practice is crucial to your career. Regardless of your clinical expertise, if you are not able to prove that you've done what a prudent professional would do in the same or similar situation, then your defense is weakened.

Mapping for a Goal

Of all the large and successful companies around today, few have been able to make a positive difference to their outcomes without a plan. Much like a care plan, a strategic plan has *steps*, which predictably outline how you can reach a desired goal. We are used to doing this for our patients, usually without thinking too much about it. When a patient presents with certain clinical signs and symptoms, we either act or react according to our critical thinking and experience. Hours and hours of care planning exercises have conditioned us to think this way. Now that we have understood the concept, it is time to apply the same type of system to the professional steps we *must* take in order to create documents that prove we have followed the nursing process.

What has made the requirement for documentation even more pressing are electronic health records. We must learn to negotiate the software that is designed to help us be more astute to the changing clinical picture that our patient is presenting, support our decisions and prompt us to act according to standards of care. This goal is in the making. Many software programs do not support this concept today, but will in the future.

How can we be proactive in our professional lives? We simply need to develop a strategic plan for our work environment. We must plan to demonstrate that the standard of care was established.

Best of all, mapping for a goal allows you to have more control over your nursing life.

A resounding theme among nurses is our job dissatisfaction: why are we so overwhelmed with work?. I believe it is because our training does not provide us with the information necessary to bring everything together: the knowledge of our clinical practice and our ability to communicate that via technology combined. This integration is key, but is often sadly missing from our day-to-day activities as care providers or as nurse leaders.

Of course most of us are happy to be nurses, a career designed to have avenues in which to grow and expand. Nurses often decide that they are not interested in remaining at the bedside their entire career. Nurses realize that being a nurse is a gateway into business, clinical, academic and/or administrative areas. These are possibilities that other professionals do not have at their disposal.

As often as nurses are ill-prepared to document according to a strategic system that tells the story of the care provided, so, too, are many of our nurse leaders ill-prepared to lead because of inadequate training. Supporting the professional process in nursing is paramount to our future as professional healthcare providers. We need to support each other in order to continue to promote our profession.

According to the American Nurses Association, nurses have a Code of Ethics. These principals are designed to guide our decision-making efforts while being licensed as a nurse. There are nine provisions that the ANA have outlined for us. Provision 4 states: "The nurse is responsible and accountable for individual nursing practice and determines the appropriate delegation of tasks consistent with the nurse obligation to provide optimum patient care." (Please see Ana.org for further details.) These provisions serve as a guide to what is expected, but the execution of these provisions remains up to the individual.

Increase Job Satisfaction, Decrease Stress

Once you map your goal, you will increase your satisfaction from work. More control increases your fulfillment and leads to less stress. But some work "off the clock" is necessary. Viewing your license as a business owner will reinforce this fact.

Putting a plan together requires an understanding of what systems or processes work and which ones require tweaking. There *is* a systematic way of putting your plan together. First, start thinking about the existing patterns in your day. Does your day begin before or after getting report? Once you leave report, are you in pretty good shape, but sometime in the middle or toward the end of your shift, do things tend to fall apart? Are there certain people or situations that make your documentation end with nonsensical entries? Think about what you would like to take control over within the constraints of your day, and that will begin the process towards gaining control. Once you take control of your documentation, you'll take control of your professionalism.

When you start to think about your purpose for a strategy plan, you might realize that the time you spend at work does not always have to be constant chaos. There are actually areas that you *can* command and control. Altering your task-to-task activities might be viewed in a negative way. Assessments, interventions, and evaluations all need to be monitored by you. This might seem kooky or even too time-consuming, but it will become second nature as you make adjustments to your system of doing things.

Sometimes, the unpopular decisions that benefit the protection of your license may cause other people to view you differently. When you integrate evidence-based practice and policy into your care, you might find other people questioning why you are so worried about doing things a certain way. Remember, in nursing there are so many ways to do the same thing, but sometimes nurses stretch the limit of what "standard of care" really means. As a professional, it is imperative that you protect your license above all else. What ultimately matters is that you know what actions are deemed appropriate to your patient and his or her situation are based both on the documented proof in his or her file and your professional experience.

What *can* you control? Well, consider the reporting process in your facility. Do you leave report feeling like you were not handed the patients in an organized way? Are there things that you wish you had asked of the nurse going off, but forgot to, or didn't realize you needed to know until that nurse had left? What about times when your patient goes for tests or therapies? Is there a way to control certain scheduled events during your shift? Can you, the nurse, have confidence that ancillary personnel will respect the requests you make? Having control over some of these things will allow you to gain control in other areas. There is a definite purpose to your strategy.

Framing

Framing your purpose begins the process of strategic planning. Much like a care plan for your patients, you should have an idea about what you want to accomplish.

Being able to articulate your goal or mission is important. When we make plans for our patients, we are looking for implementation strategies that will bring them closer to wellness. We assess their signs and symptoms in order to critically think about what we need to do for them so they will feel better. The same is true for the strategic nurse. We must build a framework in which to practice.

Understanding the conscious effort it takes to move from task to task requires us to keep track of many things at one time. We are masters at multitasking. But issues arise when we have to account for the information we are collecting and distributing throughout the shift. The patients, other professionals, and ancillary bits of communication are all factors that result in either a positive or negative outcome for our patients.

How can you multi-task and keep track of all the bits of information that tell the ultimate story of the appropriate care provided? First, begin with a framework, because a foundation is required. A foundation will empower you to anticipate some of the key factors in the equation toward mastering the nursing process. *Foundations of Nursing* by Lois White (2007) discusses this process in greater detail.

As a seminar speaker, I love meeting nurses in different cities around the nation. We are fundamentally the same. We express an innate desire to enjoy our careers. Having some control over the information we gather through the day is empowering.

Writing down information in a systematic way will become easier over time. With the EMR (Electronic Medical Records), we will be able to anticipate the language and requests of the software, once we learn the expectations along the way.

The EMR has increased the mystery to our entries. As nurses, we cannot rely on the indicators in the EMR to guide care. There are many software systems available. Since their primary function is billing, it further confirms my message. Having a personal documentation system allows you to avoid the conflicts in the EMR.

The advantage of framing your strategy will be further realized once the full EMR process is in place. The initial loading of software and navigation of the system will help your strategic approach take effect more quickly. The EMR has triggers and indicators that will not change drastically over time. The most drastic change is now. Moving forward with fine-tuning will only add to the value of your strategic plan.

With the increase in job satisfaction and decreased stress comes personal and professional growth. There is such a difference when you have a great—or even good—day at work compared to an average or terrible day. This feeling of accomplishment can only increase the production that spills over into your personal life.

I cannot imagine anyone going into nursing because she wants to feel clinically or managerially inadequate. As adults, we would rather not be reprimanded for every twist and turn. Personal growth is as much a part of strategic planning as professional growth. There are so many benefits to having a nursing framework.

Nursing is a highly competitive market and it is human to be curious about the way other nurses are managing their time. There are so many styles of nursing. There are so many things we can learn from each other. Sometimes it is difficult to ask a colleague how they get certain things done. What makes certain people more organized than others? There are nurses who seem to have all the pieces together. Are they operating on a naturally strategic plane?

Considering Superpowers

There are some people who are really gifted with a sense of direction. They do not need a global planning system (GPS) to get them to their destination. I would consider that their "superpower." Do some nurses have similar "superpowers" that enable them to drift through their assignments without having a hair out of place? As a new clinical nurse, I was perhaps the clumsiest and most disorganized person I knew. Being efficient was not one of my "superpowers." But having a strategic system really helped beef up that deficit. I cannot say that I developed this organizational "superpower" ability on my own. I was able to be much more competitive in my career once I took hold of a strategy.

There are so many places for nurses to go professionally and geographically. That is one of the benefits of being a nurse. As professionals, we are faced with growth in our jobs. Our opportunities are endless. With a system of planning, whether it is for the shift or beyond, you can have more control over your career. Having a strategy will help you gain some "superpowers" in nursing. Moving away from the feelings that your documentation can be scrutinized by the legal system and being able to concentrate on your career can bring overall personal satisfaction. Imagine your entries are a part of documentation collected that determine future patient care. Purposeful documentation is the key to avoiding litigious encounters. But it is also a major contribution to nursing in general. The collection of information shapes the nursing process.

Building a strategy requires introspection. There are many steps in the process. The checks and balances required to get it right will always remain a part of the process. It is not an immediate fix, as it will require a plan, then some minor changes to the plan. But try not to be hasty when you think something is not working. When you have a system, it will require fine-tuning for the implementation process to show its value. In medicine, when a healthcare provider prescribes a medication or treatment, often times they will begin at a low safe dose. This way they can always make changes that are incremental. Make a habit of only making changes to your plan once a week, once every two weeks, or even once a month.

It would be counterproductive to make major changes where the outcome creates a problem that is the same size or greater. Start the process and the changes with enough information that will enable you to gain control over what you can. That process, once mastered, will remain as a permanent practice throughout your career and will become something you can teach other nurses.

Strategic Planning Benefits

The benefit of a strategic plan allows you, the creator, to evaluate the system you've created. Are you achieving the documentation goals that allow you to feel comfortable once you've left your assignment? The checks and balances, re-evaluations, and the introspection required are all ways that we as nurses learn to hold ourselves accountable before anyone else can point the finger at us.

Chapter 4
How to Approach the Project

Now that you are actually thinking about putting a plan together to master documentation, it's time to consider the various approaches to building a strategic plan.

First, consider this question. Are you goal-oriented or process-oriented?

Some people function better when they have their sights set on a particular item. For example, you're scheduling a vacation. You may look at some vacation packages available during the time you'd like to travel. Planning with the end in mind will be a motivating factor, and is an example of being goal-oriented.

Some people are more process-oriented. Using the same vacation example, a process-oriented person might place more emphasis on the logistics of the vacation. You might start to think about who will travel with you. What mode of transportation would you use to get there? How long do you want to go for, and what might be your overall costs? In this case, the process of the plan grabs your attention and drives your approach to the plan.

If you are goal-oriented and contemplating how a strategic documentation system might benefit your nursing practice, you might imagine yourself leaving on time, with a peace of mind and a smile on your face. You might be able to imagine going to the gym after work because you have more energy and focus.

If you are process-oriented, you might imagine yourself going through the daily tasks with purpose and confidence: finishing one thing before beginning another, and making it a point not to get sidetracked by things that can wait.

Another benefit of this method will be not having to make excuses to people who demand your immediate attention. Paul Cornell, PhD, et. al. (2010) conducted a study on nurses workflow. This study "revealed that nurses constantly switch activities and locations in a seemingly random pattern" (p. 366). These patterns of movement make it difficult to embrace a system of purpose and predictability. The article goes on to state that when nurses are pulled from one activity to another, there is also an increase in their stress level. Studies like these further reinforce the idea that without a system for things that can be controlled and monitored, we will find ourselves defending care that was not adequately explained in the medical record.

Just as your approach to planning is important, so is the framework of your plan. There are several ways to approach your planning process. One of the wonderful things about putting a system of workflow together is the autonomy that you have. This is your plan and does not require anyone else's approval.

That being said, are you someone who really does "go with the flow" and wonders how a plan can possibly help you? Well, there is a plan for you. According to Carter McNamara at the Authenticity Consulting, LLC, firm, there is something called an "Organic" plan. This is where there is a goal, there are methods to reach that goal, but the implementation process is fluid. So, for example, pretend you have designed your strategy sheet and things are not working out as you had planned. You are able to finish on time and give a comprehensive report, but when you attempt to document, some of your indicators do not match up with the software. You might consider this enough of an accomplishment and decide not to make any more changes. The organic plan and the changes you make are fluid and will happen as you go along. Having a starting point is the most important part of this process. The development and implementation of your plan can be reorganized as you see fit. You do not stress out over every detail, because you realize that constant tweaking, whenever you feel the need, will get you to your goal of reducing the stress currently caused by documenting what you do. Your plan is an improvement and can be amended at any time.

Five steps to basic strategic planning:

1. **Identify your purpose** (similar to a mission statement)
   <u>Example</u>: *Completing documentation with comprehension, clarity, and accuracy.*
2. **Select the goals you would like to reach.**
   <u>Example</u>: *I will have an organized system of collecting information and placing appropriate values in the EMR.*
3. **Identify specific approaches to your plan.**
   <u>Example</u>: I will use a paper system to collect information, track my time and assessments. This paper can be amended at any time.
4. **Identify specific actions to implement the plan.**
   <u>Example</u>: *The plan will be used regularly and if there is something about the plan that does not meet my needs I will make incremental changes to make the plan more efficient and effective.*
5. **Monitor and update the plan**
   <u>Example</u>: *Just like a nursing care plan, I will continuously monitor my strategy to suit my mission and goals.*

Further Thoughts...

With all the thought and planning that goes into designing a system like this, how do I know that all this is worth it? There are hundreds of thousands of nurses and only a fraction of them are ever named in a lawsuit. However, so many are questioned about their documentation. You might convince yourself that something like that could only happen to someone else. But the thing about nursing is that patient assignments connect us to each other. Your documentation entry might not be the problem, but it could be associated with the problem. It's this association that you need to be aware of. Remember, the medical record is a non-fiction story. All entries are admissible. That means that if you were assigned to care for a patient who had a bad outcome, your documentation will be assessed along with the entire medical record.

Resources:

McNamara, C. (n.d.) Basic overview of various strategic planning models. Accessed February 12, 2012, from http://managementhelp.org/strategicplanning/models.htm.

Cornell, P., et. al. (2010). Transforming nursing workflow, part 1: The chaotic nature of nurses activities. *Journal of Nursing Administration, 40*(9), 366-373.

Spee, P. (2011). Strategic planning as communicative process. *Organizational Studies, 32*(9), 1217-1245. DOI: 10.1177/0170840611411387.

Chapter 5
Am I the Stakeholder?
Yes, Yes, Yes. You are # 1

Being a stakeholder simply means that you are the first person to benefit from this plan. Nursing requires your personal touch, and you are the most important stakeholder in this equation. Sorry, but I have to discuss Florence Nightingale again. Nurse Nightingale spent her free time collecting data, examining the information she collected as well as that of her colleagues. Her data collection led to one of the first concrete nursing care plans. She was able to articulate how the elements of fresh air, water, sunlight, and food contributed to soldiers' positive outcomes. We take these facts for granted, but it was the beginning of the nursing process. Nurses were able to control their patients' outcomes by manipulating their environment, recording the findings and omitting that which had a negative influence on any given patient's well being.

The information we gather while caring for patients is not primarily used to keep us out of the courtroom. The entries are used for reimbursement, practice-based evidence, other healthcare providers' information to treat and compliance with authoritative sources.

When facilities do not get reimbursed for the care you provide, it contributes to their inability to pay their bills. Healthcare cannot function if facilities are not adequately reimbursed. We must support healthcare facilities (and keep them from going under) by doing our part to contribute to the justification of the reimbursements. The diagnostic related groups (DRG) have been further delineated to increase the categorization of the procedures patients have undergone. Having our data scrutinized into minute sections increases the responsibility our documentation has. We must support the care we provide so that reimbursement will not be in question.

The entries made in the medical record are also used to determine what care works best for your patients. Social scientists spend countless hours reviewing charts to gather data in order to determine what practice-based evidence should become the standard of care. Entries are an intimate part of practice-based evidence development. If nurses do not provide this information, we will not be able to track outcomes. Healthcare practice becomes fine tuned when we include information that supports our patients' responses to interventions. (If you have a medical condition or have a loved one who requires the intervention of modern treatment, you can be assured that it is because of the established data that contributes to the best outcomes.) Collectively, we benefit from the entries explaining the care we provide to our patients. We cannot get sidetracked with being overwhelmed or believing that the electronic document will draw conclusions for us. In time, the electronic record will anticipate patients' responses, but that will only happen for us after computers assess the trends in the data.

And finally, the lawsuits. When there is a lapse of information in the medical record and the patient has a bad outcome, the records are scrutinized to determine if there is a connection. Medical malpractice lawyers are looking for causation of the injury. The entries in the record provide that information; in other words, they are the narrative notes we used to describe what the nurse was thinking and seeing. The record uses the nurse's own words to convey a message. The electronic medical record does not make that process as personal. There are questions or inquiries that must be addressed. The general consensus is that it takes longer and many of the categories are amiss. Nurses are spending time clicking boxes of a complete assessment in categories that would not normally be assessed in a particular specialty. This can be frustrating and feel like a time waster.

So what does this have to do with being a stakeholder? As nurses, our documentation dictates so many very important aspects of healthcare. We are the key contributors to what is needed, going forward, in healthcare. We hold vital information about the delivery of care and sometimes we don't share that knowledge. We have the ability to continue to be change agents—to inform and support wellness programs. If we do not make strong efforts to place a systematic approach into our day-to-day activities, we will be phased out.

The "Buying in"...

The next step in the process is "buying in" to the idea that using a strategic method to manage your assessments, interventions, communication and evaluations will actually help you. You are the only person who will benefit from this small investment of your time. Your contribution to nursing and your ability to document the care you have provided will be satisfied.

There has never been a better time to put a system like this together. Technology in healthcare is forcing us to think differently. We process information differently, we have a new sense of comfort with technology, but to an extent this is dangerous. After reading hundreds of computerized medical records, it becomes evident that there is a fundamental void. Nurses are not providing an accurate picture of what the patients look like. The information is fragmented and disjointed. It makes the documenter look ill-prepared to care for the patients.

As nurses, we are expected to follow the Nurse Practice Act outlined by our state. The Nurse Practice Act tells us how we should act as a nurse. This hasn't changed much over time, though there are additional inclusions. The role and responsibility of a nurse will become more complex as healthcare continues to mature. This roadmap, or the way we should act, remains consistent. For example, in Connecticut, the Department of Public Health has the Statutes and Regulations for nurses. Under the Connecticut General Statutes Chapter 378 is the Nurse Practice Act. This section states what a nurse who is licensed in Connecticut is expected to do.

Sec. 20-87a. Definitions. Scope of practice. (a) The practice of nursing by a registered nurse is defined as the process of diagnosing human responses to actual or potential health problems, providing supportive and restorative care, health counseling and teaching, case finding and referral, collaborating in the implementation of the total healthcare regimen, and executing the medical regimen under the direction of a licensed physician, dentist or advanced practice registered nurse. (Connecticut General Statutes)

Please refer to either your State Board of Nursing or Department of Health to read the specific guidelines that are appropriate for your state.

With all that nurses are required to do under their licensure, it makes perfect sense to practice within a personal framework using a personal strategic plan in which to guide your practice. How is one person to juggle so many responsibilities all at the same time? It is difficult to place one task above another in order of importance. We are aware of the ABC's of our CPR, but caring for a case load requires significant management of time and resources. It requires coordination and cooperation of many entities. And after all that, you are required to input your information into software that might speak a different language compared to your personal assessment practices.

As your mental strategy sheet begins to take form, the items that are most important to your clinical or managerial area will emerge. You will begin to realize what information you need to keep your documentation truthful and accurate. Some nurses are not familiar with the software and the large numbers of indicators. This makes it cumbersome to address during a documentation session. Having a documentation tool that mimics the software will allow you to contour your assessments based on the indictors presented. That is one way to design your strategy sheet, by mimicking your software.

Dwight D. Eisenhower was a strategist who stated "*Plans are nothing, planning is everything.*" He knew that planning is essential for survival. Nursing demands this, too. After all, it is in the care planning in which we learn to *care for people.*

What are the issues that are most important to you in your practice setting? Begin to think about the facets of care that are key to maintaining alignment with your state's Nurse Practice Act. Think about the indicators that are in the software that you use or that your facility is planning to use. Are there certain questions that come up frequently that you have overlooked in your assessments? This would be an important item to include. Putting a system together does not mean that you cannot do your job without one. It simply means that you will be more efficient, confident and organized if you have one. It also means that if any of your charts were ever a part of a lawsuit, you would have a stronger defense. Our nursing license guides us to follow the state's Nurses Practice Act, but it does not tell us how to do it.

The "Model of Professional Nursing Practice Regulation" is a schematic depiction of the various challenges nurses face when making decisions (*See* **Figure 5-1.**). Depicted as a pyramid, the model places our Scope of Practice, Code of Ethics, and specialty certification at the bottom. These founding principles represent the base of our professionalism. The next level is the Nurse Practice Act and the Rules and Regulations that accompany them; this is smaller—but just as important. Next are our facility's policies and procedures. This section outlines the specific requirements our institutions place on us, based on their interpretation and the restraints of their environment. And on the top of the pyramid is our Self Determination. All regulations can be used in lawsuits.

Figure 5-1. Model of Professional Nursing Practice Regulation

Strategic planning is important because it is how your personal philosophy, your personal policies and procedures and your personal code of ethics will be interpreted through effective and efficient nursing care. The end result of this framework is a document that encompasses all that is written and expected from a nursing professional.

Wow, it's starting to make sense.

Chapter 6
The Must Do Mandates

For nurses, the framework is established. We have mandated guidelines to which we must adhere because that is the interpretation of our license. Our license clearly defines our scope of practice. Building a strategy sheet must contain the mission, values and goals for you, the designer, but just like your facility, you should also create personal policies and procedures that will guide your care. Staying mindful of the mandates required should help keep things moving.

Mandates are those things that must be done for our patients. There are formal and informal mandates. For example, in your facility, there might be a union. Unions have mandates that must be followed. Unions have elected officials who serve terms. The nominees and the process of campaigning can be considered an informal mandate. As nurses, we also have informal mandates. Informal mandates that allow us to follow the rules in our own way.

Nurse Susan B. Hassmiller, PhD, is the Robert Wood Johnson Foundation Senior Adviser for Nursing. She was interviewed in 2011 by Nurse Christine T. Kovner, PhD, in *Nursing Economics*. This article outlines a report Dr. Hassmiller prepared for released at the Institute of Medicine. The report is entitled "The Future of Nursing: Leading Change, Advancing Health." It discusses recommendations for the future of nursing. As discussed in the Nurse Informatics article, there are four recommendations outlined:

1. Nurses should practice to the full extent of their education and training.
2. Nurses should achieve higher levels of education and training through an improved education system that promotes seamless academic progression.

3. Nurses should be full partners, with physicians and other healthcare professionals, in redesigning healthcare in the United States.
4. Effective workforce planning and policy making require better data collection and information infrastructure.

These could be considered informal mandates. Nursing is an ever-evolving entity. We are at a crossroads of transition due to technological explosion, healthcare reform, budget cuts, chronic diseases, and increased and decreased patient awareness—the list goes on. We cannot afford to practice nursing the same way we have been doing it. The expectations in healthcare are changing and keeping current is expected.

If your former patients have had bad outcomes and they thought it was negligence, they might take their complaints to a plaintiff attorney. The lawyer will study the record looking for entries to strengthen a case against your facility. Each entry, when read collectively, is used to tell the story about the care provided. Most medical malpractice attorneys are not healthcare providers. They are using the medical record and their knowledge of the law to determine if there has been a deviation in the standard of care. What you concentrate on and what you write about are done based on mandates. The way your thoughts are organized and the follow through provided in the documentation are your informal mandates.

There are mandates in healthcare that are easy to decipher. For example, you know that an assessment will include: temperature, pulse, respiration and blood pressure. These mandates, as simple and elementary as they may seem, are sometimes missing in the health record. Having neglected to include these in your work product can make it difficult to prove that you assessed them. But that is stating the obvious.

Other mandated pieces of information might be tests, labs, services provided, results, conversations and reactions to treatments. But is the expectation for your documentation to reiterate what is already there? No, absolutely not. If the information is already in the medical record, then you should not have to repeat it in your entries.

The problem comes in when the information that is already in the system, coupled with your information, lacks congruency. Just because essential information can be found in the same record does not mean the nurse has integrated the information into practice. This is where critical thinking comes in, otherwise known as your informal mandates. This can be interpreted as the way you carry out the formal mandates and is key when creating a strategic plan for your nursing care.

Granted, the electronic record will assist us with clinical decision-making support. However, as nurses, our judgment of care will always be in question, not that of the software. Your ability to recognize information that needs to be addressed in your entries becomes easier over time, but might never happen if there isn't a systematic approach to tracking information.

Another example might be a conversation you've had with another healthcare member. Suppose your patient requires the services of a physical therapist. Perhaps that therapist, during their assessment and intervention with the patient, learns that the patient has been having an adverse reaction to a medication that you administered for the first time. As we know, patients disclose different pieces of information to various healthcare providers, and this contributes to the entire healthcare story. When the therapist speaks to you about this, does that conversation belong in the medical record? Or does that interaction you've had with the therapist warrant follow up on your part?

Unfortunately, that depends on other pieces of information, like the medication, the side effect, the patient and the therapist. Without a formal process of critically thinking about all of your collected information, not getting the accurate story in the medical record could have adverse consequences. Of course, you are always critically thinking, but do not forget the haphazard events that can occur during clinical practice. As easy as it is to think critically, it is just as easy to get pulled away from that thought into another.

Strategic planning using the knowledge of your formal and informal mandates will further provide the framework necessary to keep current with the expectations under your nursing license. Consider the mandates of your job. Do you work with a patient population where the patients require assessment of their fluid and electrolyte balance? Or does their skin have specific telltale signs that you should be assessing closely? In many of the medical malpractice cases that I review, the patient is presenting with low-grade temperatures, mild symptoms of pain and malaise. Are these some of the subtle signs and symptoms that you should be tracking during your shift?

Resources:

Kovner, C. & Spetz, J. (2011). The future of nursing: An interview with Susan B. Hassmiller, *Nursing Economics, 29*(1), 32-43.

Bryson, J. (2004). *Strategic planning for public and non-profit organizations*, 4th edition. Hoboken, NJ: Wiley Publication.

Chapter 7
Do I Need a Mission Statement? Yes, Yes, Yes.

Having a personal mission statement might sound "hokey-pokey," but it's not. Nurses are people who must run their own businesses. Like it or not, we are business owners; our business is providing services under our licenses. There are not many industries like ours. We own nurse staffing companies, services and product companies, consulting firms, we write books and speak publicly, and many of us work as per diem or agency employees. These are all examples of being self-employed. And even if you are employed by a facility, you are working there because of your credentials. Having a mission statement continues to shape your foundation as a nurse.

Mission statements are constructed using all the tools we have already talked about. Why have a strategic plan, methods for growing a strategic plan and the mandates necessary to accomplish these goals? The mission statement sums up the core values leading you to create a professional, yet personal, statement of purpose.

In the book *Strategic Planning for Public and Nonprofit Organizations,* a mission statement is explained to clarify an organization's purpose, or why it does what it does (Bryson; Jossey-Bass, 2004). There have been several times during my nursing career that I have questioned the authorities as well as my own reason for nursing. I wondered why certain things are done certain ways. The policies and procedures a facility adopts come from the mandates at the state and federal level. The facilities create their own mission statement that helps guide their goals and objectives. Without these, they might be failing at taking care of patients safely and within the standards of practice. The mission statement also allows outsiders to understand what they are trying to accomplish. It can be thought of as a mantra, a slogan, or a motto. Any sentence that sums up the reason you decide is what makes things come together.

Missions, mantras, slogans or mottos are not fixed for your

entire nursing career. They can be fluid statements that change according to you. Just like the Code of Ethics in nursing, which is a set of provisions that changes because the healthcare climate changes, so can be your statement of purpose.

As leaders and authoritative sources in your own right, having a mission statement is a simple as stating your case. Here are some examples of mission statements:

McDonald's Restaurant. "McDonald's vision is to be the world's best quick service restaurant experience. Being the best means providing outstanding quality, service, cleanliness, and value, so that we make every customer in every restaurant smile." (McDonald's Restaurant, 2012)

Google. "To organize the world's information and make it universally accessible and useful." (Google, 2011)

OSHA. "To assure the safety and health of America's workers by setting and enforcing standards; providing training, outreach, and education; establishing partnerships; and encouraging continual improvement in workplace safety and health." (OSHA, 2005)

American Red Cross. "The American Red Cross, a humanitarian organization led by volunteers and guided by its Congressional Charter and the Fundamental Principles of the International Red Cross and Red Crescent Movement, will provide relief to victims of disaster and help people prevent, prepare for, and respond to emergencies." (American Red Cross, 2012)

These examples of mission statements summarize the reasons companies exist. They create a tangible statement of purpose. If you have had any experience with any of the companies listed above, you might agree that their service matches their mission.

It helps for you to have a statement of personal service.

It does not have to be long; for example, Google's statement is one sentence. I realize that the mission statements and/or statements of purpose used here are all business models. Nurses, collectively and individually, are service providers, which isn't all that different. Having a mission statement of your own will provide you with the foundation needed in order to provide proficient service to your patients. This mind set will assist you in case you are ever a defendant in a medical malpractice issue.

Think about your purpose for providing nursing care that is within the standard of practice. Are you driven to make people move closer to wellness while providing safety along the way? Or are you more focused on being a teacher and leader? There are so many ways to think about your mission. It all has to do with providing safe care according to the mandates.

For the record, my mission statement for this book is: To provide information to empower nurses when documenting facts in the medical record.

Now, jot down your own mission statement:

Resources:

Bryson, J.M., Jossey-Bass (2004). *Strategic planning for public and nonprofit organizations: A guide to strengthening and sustaining organizational achievement.* p 102. John Wiley & Sons, San Francisco, CA.

Mission & Values. (n.d.). Accessed January 29, 2012, from www.aboutmcdonalds.com/mcd/our_company.html.

Vision. (n.d.). Accessed March 26, 2012 from http://www.google.com/about/company.

U.S. Department of Labor. (2005, para 1). Small business safety and health management series OSHA 2209-02R. Accessed January 29, 2012, from www.osha.gov/Publications/smallbusiness/small-business.html.

Bryson, J. (2004). *Strategic planning for public and non-profit organizations*, 4th edition. Hoboken, NJ: Wiley Publication.

Chapter 8

Factors to Consider
When Formulating your Actual Plan

What does a strategy sheet look like? In the mind's eye, it can take many forms. The items that it must include are the most important ones.

Documentation might seem like a "no-brainer" since we are in the process of complete automation. But that really only complicates things. We think that the systems, which provide almost mindless entries, will cover all the bases. Those intense question and answer sessions only serve to confuse the end result.

The electronic systems are working hard to create pathways that support the clinician. But we are not there yet. Not all systems are designed the same and not all offer 100% support for your cases. With that in mind, please note that we can, to some extent, lean on the systems in order to prompt thought and insight. But we cannot rely on them 100% to draw conclusions about our patients and their responses to our interventions.

In addition, we cannot allow other nurses' entries to impact our own assessments. Cutting and pasting one entry to the next might demonstrate to the reader that each nurse is simply following the assessment of the previous caregiver.

Our patients are moving along a continuum and we are mandated to assess and document interventions as they occur in real time. In addition to all that, the changes that occur from shift to shift are so difficult to keep up with that regulatory agencies are involved in our communication process, hence: "handing off".

A *strategy sheet* should allow you to scan the information and tell a story about your patient's response to the interventions. There are many interventions that you might carry out during a given shift. Keeping up with them becomes cumbersome and, at times, dangerous. Conversations with others regarding your patients and the healthcare process might need to be included in your documentation. How is the average mind expected to accommodate all this information without a tool? The end result is a more efficient "hand-off".

The construction of a strategy sheet requires a couple more regimented items to be effective. A brief discussion regarding internal and external factors is necessary. An external factor is something you cannot change. It is similar to a mandate, but is based on a policy or regulation that your facility institutes. Although the Joint Commission Center for Transforming Healthcare (JCCTH) made a statement about the "handing off" process, your facility has instituted its own interpretation of that activity. This external factor must be taken into consideration when designing a strategy sheet.

The law views the same factors in a litigious matter as the regulators. Lawyers look to the regulators to prove if a healthcare provider has deviated from the standard of care. The regulators, for example, would be the Center for Medicare and Medicaid, The Joint Commission, and the Agency for Healthcare.

Research and Quality

When documenting with the law in mind, policy interpretation is the key. An unblemished license means using the policy statements provided by your state and federal guidelines. Placing emphasis on who, what, why and where are internal factors. But how you define them requires effort and critical thought.

Internal factors are things we can control. To some extent, we control our scheduling, our specialty and our venue. We also control how we get and receive reports.

When you are getting a report, you are the *receiver*. You are actively listening to the nurse who has taken care of your patient for the last shift. You are listening for all the information to formulate a plan of continued action. Some things are more important than others, but all information exchanged should be used to give you enough information to safely and effectively care for that patient.

When you are the *sender*, your responsibility is to actively engage the oncoming nurse with the pertinent events that occurred during your shift. The response to interventions, vital signs, responses to illness and conversations that made a difference to the outcome of your patient's path towards wellness should be included. Using inflections and emphasis to help communicate information that the receiver should understand are important contributions to the process. I realize the "handing off" process instituted by the JCCTH has constraints, but, again within those constraints come our personal interpretations.

JCCTH has determined that "80% of serious medical errors involve miscommunication between caregivers when patients are transferred or handed-off." (Joint Commission Center for Transforming Healthcare, 2011)

As one of the contributing factors to sentinel events, this concept of planning your care is crucial. Considered a National Patient Safety Goal (NPSG) because of the relationship to serious medical errors, developing a system that you design could not have come at a better time. Tracking events along a timeline is a significant component to keeping your care from being questioned.

The acronym SHARE developed by the JCCTH means:

S – Standardize critical content, including
- Providing details of the patient's history to the receiver
- Emphasizing key information about the patient when speaking with the receiver
- Synthesizing patient information from separate sources before passing it on to the receiver

H – Hardwire within your system, including
- Developing standardized forms, tool and methods, such as checklists
- Using a quiet workplace or setting that is conducive to sharing information about a patient

- Stating expectations about how to conduct a successful hand-off
- Identifying new and existing technologies to assist in making the hand-off successful

A – Allow opportunities to ask questions, including
- Using critical skills when discussing a patient's care
- Sharing and receiving information as an interdisciplinary team (e.g., pit crew)
- Expecting contact information about the patient from the sender
- Exchanging contact information in the event there are any additional questions
- Scrutinizing and questioning the data

R – Reinforce quality and measurement, including
- Demonstrating leadership commitment to successful hand-off
- Holding staff accountable for managing a patient's care
- Monitoring compliance with use of standardize forms, tools and methods for hand-offs
- Using data to determine a systematic approach for improvement

E – Educate and coach, including
- Teaching staff what constitutes a successful hand-off
- Standardizing training on how to conduct a hand-off
- Providing real-time performance feedback to staff
- Making successful hand-offs an organization priority

Whether you decide to use index cards, colored paper, a spiral notebook or an electronic document does not matter. What matters is your approach to the multitude of factors that need to be included.

The effort by JCCTH to improve safety further dissected the issues and found the problems can be divided into three categories: General, Sending and Receiving.

The following are considered failures in the system:

General:
1. Culture does not promote successful hand-off, e.g., lack of teamwork and respect
2. Expectations between sender and receiver differ
3. Ineffective communication methods, e.g. verbal, recorded, bedside, written
4. Timing of physical transfer of the patient and the hand-off are not in sync
5. Inadequate amount of time provided for successful hand-off
6. Interruptions occur during hand-off
7. Lack of standardized procedures in conducting successful hand-off, e.g., SBAR
8. Inadequate staffing at certain times of the day or week to accommodate successful hand-off
9. Patient not included during hand-off

Sender:
1. Sender provides inaccurate or incomplete information, e.g., medication list, DNR, concerns/issues, contact information
2. Sender, who has little knowledge of the patient, is handing patient off to the receiver
3. Sender unable to provide up-to-date information, e.g., lab test, radiology reports, because not enough information is available at the time of the hand-off
4. Sender unable to contact the receiver who will be taking care of the patient in a timely manner
5. Inability of sender to follow up with the receiver if additional information needs to be shared

Receiving:
1. Receiver has competing priorities and is unable to focus on transferred patient
2. Receiver unaware of patient transfer

3. Inability for receiver to follow up with sender if additional information is needed
4. Lack of responsiveness by receiver
5. Receiver has little knowledge of patient being transferred

(The Joint Commission Center for Transforming Healthcare, 2011)

There are so many factors to take into consideration when planning and plotting a strategy sheet. When you are the receiver, it is difficult to know what information is missing when you are not familiar with the patient. How are you supposed to know what the sender should be telling you? Often times, you have questions for the nurse after they have left. Does a contact number where he or she can be reached belong on your strategy sheet?

Since the system is designed to support the process, there are so many variables you can use to create an efficient tool that provides a framework your nursing practice.

Here are just a few things to consider when thinking about your strategy sheet:

Skeleton/Back drop
  Size of the sheet
  Weight of the paper
  Color of the paper
  Symbols/codes/abbreviations
  Timeline – across the top or down the side or none at all
  Facility Numbers
  Columns or boxes or both
  Excel or Word

Patient Demographics
  Location / Family contact
  HCP/Teams ➡ Contact info
  Took Report from ➡ Contact info

Substance
  Diagnosis upon admission - what are s/s of diagnosis?
  V/S trends / dx specific/ assessment specific
  New Medication/Treatment/Response
  HCP visit to the patient
  Tests/labs – results
  What's new since this shift?
  What did your patient say?
  What's coming up for next shift?
  What services is the patient receiving?
  Did you talk to anyone today about your patient?
  What is your general impression of the patient?

Write your story for the reader.

Resources:

Joint Commission. (n.d). Facts about hand-off communication.
    Accessed March 26, 2012 ,http://www.
    centerfortransforminghealthcare.org/projects/detail.
    aspx?Project=1.

Tackling hand-off communications. [Journal Article]. (2011, January).
    Hospital Peer Review. 36(1), 5-6.

Chapter 9
Tools of the Trade

As healthcare becomes more automated, your personal systems can serve as the checks and balances for the various pieces of technology that you are required to use.

There are multiple factors to keep in mind, such as the federal and state requirements and Joint Commissions handing off policy statement and their interpretation of these things and then you have your clinical policies. Along with the Nursing Code of Ethics, it seems like there are so many entities to satisfy. Designing a tool that allows you to stay within the parameters set up this far are important for documentation that keeps you away from litigation.

But what if a patient you took care of had a bad outcome and your documentation was included with that of nurses who were being scrutinized? Suppose the patient's bad outcome occurred just after you took care of her. Suppose you developed a tool that allowed you to keep track of the patient's signs and symptoms of disease, your interventions and the hand-off process. You would think that all avenues had been taken care of to protect your license, but it's possible that they hadn't.

When a patient has a bad outcome and they seek the representation of legal counsel, the attorney has to determine if the four elements of a lawsuit have been met. The four elements are duty, breath of duty, damages and causation. This basically means there is a *legal relationship* between you and the facility. Once you accept the assignment and the patient has a bad outcome, the law takes the allegations to determine if you have caused the damages. Once these factors have been established and the lawsuit is filed, there are many responsibilities the defense and plaintiff teams have when sorting out the facts of the case. You will have a chance to speak to the care you've provided during deposition. When you are deposed, the opposing attorney will ask you questions in the presence of a court reporter and your attorney. This question and answer session allows you to talk about things that you did that were not written down. For example, suppose you are caring for a patient with an abdominal drain. You've noticed that the drain collects fluid when the patient lays on her right side. You have instructed the patient to remain on her right side to facilitate drainage and given her the rationales. None of this is documented.

Fast forward to the following shift. You have handed off your patients and made it a point to tell the oncoming nurse that this patient with the abdominal drain has been given specific instructions to remain laying on her right side to accommodate the drainage system. The nurse documents that the patient was received on her left side and the drain was clogged. All attempts had been made to clear the line. Nothing worked, the physician was called, and the line was pulled and replaced. This resulted in a systemic infection resulting in a prolonged hospitalization and ongoing complications.

How does deposition help you further explain the care provided? Deposition allows you to explain things that you did not write down. Since it is done during a question and answer session, you will have an opportunity to talk about the systems you use when caring for patients and handing them off.

One of deposition's goals is to talk specifically about the standards of care. Did you, in this situation, do all the clinical things that another nurse in this same situation would have done. Yes, you did. You knew that the line drained effectively on the right side and you instructed the patient to remain on her right side, because you use a personal tracking system to denote all the care and interventions you provide. Just because you did not write it down does not necessarily mean you didn't do it, because there really are some things that cannot be written down. But a systemic approach to your care is so crucial to your innocence that keeping your personal accounts of the events gives you the opportunity to explain them in the medical record.

©∧∨∞≠/ ▪ ①⊘□

⟨⟩≈≅•○◉

■❖★◆☑☒□♪

#α β γ ω ς

□□Ξ Π Ρ Σ Δ

What symbols and abbreviations could you use as parts of your strategy sheet?

A symbol might mean nothing to an outsider, but everything to you, the documenter. That's why you should assign symbols to your tracking sheet.

What are some catch phrases you could use to include more information about the care and responses provided?

Resources:

Austin, S. (2011). Stay out of court with proper documentation. *Nursing 2011, 41*(4), 24-29.

March, A. *(2011)*. The mock trial: A collaborative interdisciplinary approach to understanding legal and ethical issues. *Nurse Educator. 36*(2), 66-69.

Mannix, M. E. (2011, March 7). National patient safety awareness week. *Joint Commission Resources.* Accessed March 7, 2011 http://jamessproject.com/blog/jfgi-its-patient-safety-awareness-week/

National patient safety current awareness (2012). Accessed March 26, 2012 http://www.npsf.org/National Patient Safety Foundation

Chapter 10

SWOC – The Strengths, Weaknesses, Opportunities and Challenges of your Plan

Since it's become more evident that there are many challenges to creating a document like this, it is important to continue to organize the tool using one more component, keeping in mind the authoritative sources as your backdrop. Being familiar with your strengths, weaknesses, opportunities and challenges allows the strategic process to have more value. Being able to know where more of your energies should go will help you streamline your documentation process. This document can always be amended; after all, healthcare is fluid and your process of gathering information needs to keep pace with your professional demands. What's important today might not be important tomorrow.

What are your strengths as a clinician? What are the strengths of your organization and the people around you? Are you the type of nurse who can recall information easily? Is your strength in being a people person, getting patients to do things other nurses cannot? The strengths of a nurse are so varied. There are nurses who seem to get along very well with all staff members. They know where to get certain things and who to call. Thinking about them can help you design a sheet that has the information you need at the tips of your fingers.

First, list your strengths:

_____

_____

_____

Your weaknesses also need to be considered. It really helps to know where you need a little extra attention. I can recall working on a unit where I was always forgetting equipment needed for a procedure. I'm not certain if it was because of the location of my rooms or the location of the supply room. Blaming the logistics of the facilities and complaining about something that I had no control over seemed pointless, so I decided to try and gather all my equipment at the beginning of my shift. I thought that maybe if I wasn't in a hurry just before the procedure, I'd be more organized, I would be able to do so without having to go back and forth multiple times. By doing this I could create some organization in my day. That was the factor that could change the equation, thus removing unnecessary steps from my day.

Nurses have been known to walk between four and ten miles per shift or more. I was probably walking more before I removed the unnecessary steps by organizing what I could control at the beginning of my shift. I would do a quick scan of the labs and tests I needed to do for the shift and make that a shift priority. It sounds elementary, but it saved me many steps.

What are the opportunities you have or that are available to you? If you are unfamiliar with the software used to create your documentation, would it be possible to get a blank print out? This might be an opportunity. Use what you have in your environment and make it work in your favor.

List your weaknesses:

Being able to recognize that nursing is not a stagnant profession and that it offers many opportunities is valuable. The Nursing Code of Ethics supports all the opportunities a nurse could imagine, reminding us that respect and commitment will continue to move us forward. Opportunities could be the technology that you use or the social support that you get at work.

List your opportunities:

_____

_____

_____

Challenges might be easier to come up with, given the amount of things being juggled simultaneously. The demands and expectations of the healthcare environment and the ever-changing requirements are two examples of challenges. Challenges, like the demands of healthcare are usually outside of our control. People we don't get along with at work could be a challenge. Things that make us feel insecure or threatened might be considered challenges.

List your challenges:

_____

_____

_____

According to Lee, et. al. (2000) we should look at our list of strengths, weaknesses, opportunities and challenges and realize that the relationships between and among them confirm a pattern. For example, Lee et. al. (2000) states that if you combine the four factors, you can see the dynamics that arise and further use the relationship to your advantage.

When you examine your strengths and opportunities and combine their effects, you can capitalize on new opportunities. When you look at your strengths and challenges, you can use your strengths to minimize your challenges or the threats you feel. When you look at your weaknesses against your opportunities, you might be able to use those opportunities to conquer your weaknesses. And finally, when you take time to examine your weaknesses and challenges, you can create a defensive strategy and function in an anticipatory manner.

Table 10-1. SWOC Factor Relationships

Strengths	+	Challenges	=	Strengths can minimize challenges
Weaknesses	+	Opportunities	=	Opportunities can conquer weaknesses
Weaknesses	+	Challenges	=	Create defensive strategies and function with anticipation

Resources:

Lee, S., Lo, K., Leung, R., & Andrew, S. (2000). Strategy formulation for vocational education: Integrating swot analysis, balanced scorecard, qfd methodology and mbnqa education criteria. *Managerial Auditing Journal, 15*(8), 407-423.

Part 2: The Not-So-Serious Side

Chapter 11
The GYN Clinic

"It's Wednesday and you know what that means," remarks Lauren at the front desk. She's organizing all the charts for the day. She usually takes all the patients Dr. Drigger is seeing before lunch and organizes them according to the patients' scheduled appointments. "Wednesday is Dr. Drigger's really busy day and she has some of the most difficult patients scheduled today."

"Who would you consider her most difficult patient today? All her patients love her, you know that," says Stormie, the RN who usually works in the chemo room, but who is working with Dr. Drigger today assisting with patient procedures and follow up appointments. There was a time when Stormie worked with Dr. Drigger all the time doing procedures, but Dr. Drigger's attitude when she was under a lot of pressure made Stormie very uncomfortable, to the point of wanting to cry. She would go home very upset, explaining to her family the horrible things Dr. Drigger would say to her. It had been a few months since the last episode and Dr. Drigger's regular nurses were not in today. Stormie knew the systems in and outside the chemo room, so that's why she had been asked to float and assist with the clinic patients today.

"You might think they all love her, but when I'm sitting out here, checking people in and the hall is quiet, I can hear conversations that would make you want to buy extra malpractice insurance. There are some very angry patients here at our gynoncology clinic. These women have not only lost their health, but many of them suffer with the loss of consortium."

"Their what?" asks Stormie.

"You know, their ability to have relations with their partners," explained Lauren.

Stormie wasn't that surprised to hear that some of the patients didn't like Dr. Drigger's bedside manner. But the truth was, Dr. Drigger was a very skilled physician and no one could deny that.

"Oh, that. Lauren, you're so smart, when are you going to sit for the bar? You finished law school last year, right?"

"I'm waiting to get the nerve up. Now shhh, here comes Mrs. Wargo".

"Hello, Mrs. Wargo, you look really nice today. Has it stopped raining?"

"No," replies, Mrs. Wargo. "Here are my papers. Is the doctor here yet?"

"No," replies Stormie, "but I can get you checked in and settled in a room, so you don't have to wait out here. Follow me".

Stormie walks Mrs. Wargo into an exam room, takes a brief history and instructs her to don a hospital gown. Before leaving, Stormie reviews her medical record and asks how things are going.

"Not very well," replies Mrs. Wargo. "I have a pain down there all the time. Something is leaking. I change pads at least four times a day. I called Dr. Drigger's office and left several messages. Finally I get a call back from her PA, who tells me to come in. The doctor thinks that I might need to have more work done. There might be a leak at the flap.

"I am so tired of this," continues Mrs. Wargo. "I don't know what to tell you. I really don't want another surgery. I don't want to have that part of my body continuously *poked* and *prodded* by anyone except my husband.

"And speaking of that," Mrs. Wargo continued, "my husband won't even look at me while I'm dressed anymore, not to mention when I'm naked. Today, he dropped me off and said our son's school called with an emergency. Sometimes I find it hard to believe him. I think he might have turned to someone else for company.

"Do you know this has been going on for 18 months? Oh, Stormie, I've known you since before this whole thing started. What am I doing wrong? Does Dr. Drigger really know what she's doing? I go from thinking she's helping me to being downright angry at her. Sometimes I think she has me coming back over and over again so she can bill my insurance company. I am so mad at this whole thing, I wish I could have some control, but I don't." Tears are rolling down Mrs. Wargo's cheeks.

Stormie is still. She's trying to use all the interpersonal skills she learned all those years back in nursing school. The tissues are close by; Stomie grabs the tissues, hands them to Mrs. Wargo and places a hand on her shoulder. "Mrs. Wargo, I am sorry to hear that; Dr. Drigger is so good at what she does and is so thoughtful, I'm sure that she will see you today and get things moving in the right direction."

After a pause, Stormie asks, "Is there anything I can get for you while you're waiting? A magazine, or a cup of water?"

"No." Replies Mrs. Wargo.

Stormie makes her way back to the check-in desk to see if any other patients have shown up. She stops to talk to Lauren.

"So, Lauren, who are some unhappy patients of Dr. Drigger?"

"Well, take Mrs. Wargo for example. Last time, she was here talking on her cell phone and she was saying that she thinks Dr. Drigger must have done something wrong to her. She was so mad that she walked out without seeing the doctor. She said things like 'everyone thinks she's such a good doctor and she really isn't.' Dr. Drigger needs to take special care of that one. Mrs. Wargo even told another patient that if her situation weren't so complicated, she would go to another doctor."

"Oh. What do you think happened?"

"I don't know," replies Lauren, "but Mrs. Wargo said something about not being afraid to hold someone accountable if she doesn't get the best care possible."

"All right then, let me go and check on her. I'll take good care of her today; I always do anyway."

Stormie stops in to see Mrs. Wargo on her way to another patient. "Dr. Drigger isn't here yet, but she's expected any moment now."

"Thanks," replies Mrs. Wargo.

Dr. Drigger rushes in twenty-five minutes later. She is

ready to get to work, as always. Dr. Drigger is very dedicated to her practice. She's written several published papers and has speaking engagements all over the country.

She begins her day with Mrs. Wargo. Before Dr. Drigger enters the room, she glances at the latest note and phone call entered by the PA. These entries cause her to take a seat and review the chart more carefully. When she enters the room, Dr. Drigger is looking for Stormie so they can examine the patient together. Since Stormie is with another patient, Dr. Drigger enters the room alone, thinking this might be a good time to clear the miscommunication with the patient.

They are behind closed doors for about 15 minutes. Mrs. Wargo's voice is audible outside the hallway with inflections that express panic. When Dr. Drigger emerges, she looks to Stormie for help. "I went ahead and examined her. Let's get her ready and do this as soon as possible." She writes orders for a mild sedative and asks for the room to be set up for the procedure.

When Mrs. Wargo is prepped, legs raised in the stirrups and the doctor has assumed her position, Stormie reviews the chart one last time and realizes that the consent has expired. In this facility, the consent is valid for five days after it is signed. She counts on her fingers twice, and realizes it has been seven days. Stormie looks over to Mrs. Wargo. Her eyes are heavy and her head is moving from side to side. She is relaxed from the medication and there is no one with her to consent. Stormie next looks to the doctor. Dr. Drigger's face is buried under the sheet that provides privacy for the patient. She gestures to Dr. Drigger and points to the consent and date.

"Oh, brother," Dr. Drigger whispers under her breath. "Quick, get the husband on the phone and get a verbal consent from him."

Stormie uses the phone at the far end of the room to call Mr. Wargo. "Dr. Drigger, there is no answer. I left a message."

"Oh what the hell," states Dr. Drigger, "lets do it anyway, she implied to me that she wants this done and I'll have her sign as soon as the medicine wears off and she has the capacity to sign."

Stormie looks at the doctor "Dr. Drigger, I don't agree with this".

The process of informed consent is unavoidable if you work in a hospital or surgical care center or really any facility where invasive procedures are done. Physicians use this document to make certain they have permission to invade a person's body before a procedure.

But what purpose does that document serve? Who does it protect? Does it protect a patient or a physician, and what role does the nurse play in this legal and ethical relationship? Courts are full of lawsuits where patients have a negative healthcare experience and feel like the physician did not communicate the unforeseen outcome.

In Minnesota 1905, Anna Mohr (Mohr v. Williams) went to see her doctor. He determined she had a problem with her right ear. She agreed to undergo surgical intervention for her right ear. While she was under anesthesia, Dr. Williams found the left ear to be the problem. He performed surgery on her left ear without her permission.

Mrs. Mohr sued and won her case. The court decided that her physician should have informed her about all of the circumstances surrounding the surgery, because the law views touching a person against their will as battery. If a healthcare provider touches someone in a way that the person had not agreed with the healthcare provider about, that person (patient) can sue (Paterick, 2008).

The language in the informed consent documents outlines that the physician (or healthcare provider) performing the procedure has communicated specific information. It basically states that there should be full disclosure of what the patient's problem is, what choices are available to fix the problem, the most prudent choice, what could happen if the procedure is not done and what could happen as a result of the procedure. Which seems simple enough, right? So how could anyone get this wrong? (Paterick, 2008)

It is the modernization of treatment modalities that causes so much controversy. The conversations between patients and their physicians are not always witnessed. In a court of law, the truth cannot just rest on the conversation recalled since it can be years between the event and the deposition or trial. The surrounding circumstances contribute to finding the innocence or guilt in a lawsuit involving the failure to consent.

Nurses are such poignant professional in healthcare. We provide the most intimate care to our patients. Yet studies show that patients often do not know who their nurses are and what role we play in their care.

Before we can appreciate a patient's ability to make a very serious decision about the direction their healthcare should take, let's take a look at the fundamental information we think a patient should understand about the actual course of treatment they are getting. There was a study conducted by O'Leary, et. al. (2010). They were looking at patients' knowledge of their care plans and the people assigned to take care of them. They collected data from 240 patients, interviewed patients on their second hospital day, and asked them questions about their care. For example, they asked the patients what their medical diagnosis was, what medication they were taking and what tests they were undergoing. In their conclusion, they felt that a large percentage of their patients did not understand their plan of care or a majority of the elements within the care plan. (O'Leary, et. al. 2010). There were some variables for teaching hospitals versus facilities with hospitals and they did take healthcare literacy into consideration. The study concluded that physicians and nurses need to be aware that patients learn at a much slower rate than we teach. This has significant effects when patients are asked to make decisions about invasive procedures or follow discharge instructions.

If patients don't understanding their plan of treatment by the second day, it might mean that they do not understand significant information communicated by their physician or designee. Nurses are in a perfect position to facilitate the process of informed consent. This is not to say that nurses are at risk of being involved with a lawsuit. Nurses are not responsible for obtaining the informed consent because we are not performing the procedure, but there are times when the circumstances surrounding the consent process may involve a nurse.

Suppose a patient has been medicated with a narcotic or an anti-insomniac and the physician has asked you to wake the patient because the patient needs to sign the consent before the morning. There are times when nurses are part of determining if a consent process was done ethically. Nurses can assist patients in understanding the information because, traditionally, we spend more time with our patients. The time we spend with them would be best utilized if we engage in conversations that elevate their health literacy levels.

Physicians are very skilled in explaining healthcare procedures and outcomes. Part of their training and education comes from teaching information to their classmates. Like nurses, they are educators too. In modern day medicine, our patients are consumers of health. They may not solely rely on the physician to learn about their health deficit, they seek books, blogs, listservs and life experience to gather information. Physicians are serving more as consultants in the healthcare advice and informed consent process. (Paterick, 2008) With this thought, physicians have to strike a balance between giving patients enough information to make an informed decision while maintaining their professionalism and following the standards of care.

Now that patients are such an integral part of our healthcare system, they have been given the responsibility to make important decisions about their care. They may want to sue physicians over issues such as the failure to consent, but they now take some responsibility for their actions. Patients are not always comfortable taking on more responsibility. It has become more of a burden for many. This is why the patient advocacy element in healthcare has become more prominent.

Nursing documentation, when involved in an informed consent process, needs to take into account the patient's ability to comprehend the information. Patients with low healthcare literacy will need more time to comprehend. Perhaps deciding on the most important aspect of their healthcare will reinforce what you should also be concentrating on.

According to Center for Healthcare Strategies (CHCS, 2011) healthcare literacy is defined as "the degree to which individuals have the capacity to obtain, process, and understand basic health information and services needed to make appropriate health decisions." Basic information is most difficult for people with chronic illnesses, but regardless of the level of literacy, people who are injured because they feel information has not communicated effectively might seek legal representation if their experience in the healthcare system ends unsatisfactorily. Be very aware of the level of literacy your patients have. Health literacy is similar to literacy. You might see someone sitting down holding an open book and turning pages or they might be holding an e-reader, but that does not mean they are reading. The same can be said for the explanations you give to patients or the information a physician gives to a patient about an invasive procedure. Information should be written in language people of all levels can understand. Supplemental information in the form of videos, pictures and tapes can help people better understand the health information. Center for Medicare and Medicaid (CMS) and Joint Commission (JC) have strict policies regarding informed consent. Both Web sites are open to the public.

There are several informed consent guidelines written within the CMS website. They provide guidance to be used by the facilities wishing to obtain reimbursement for services. They also explain the state survey tools used when making site visits. The guidelines are written to help facilities follow the proper protocols, but they can be difficult to interpret. CMS provides further direction by including an "Interpretive Guidelines" section to further explain the requirements.

According to CMS:
"The primary purpose of the informed consent process for surgical services is to ensure that the patient, or the patient's representative, is provided information necessary to enable him/her to evaluate a proposed surgery before agreeing to the surgery. Typically, this information would include potential short and longer-term risks and benefits to the patient of the proposed intervention, including the likelihood of each, based on the available clinical evidence, as informed by the responsible practitioner's professional judgment. Informed consent must be obtained, and the informed consent form must be placed in the patient's medical record, prior to the procedure, except in the case of emergency surgery." (CMS, p.)

The following guidelines explain Informed Consent
42 CFR 482.51(b)(2) – For Surgical Informed Consent
42 CFR 482.24 (c) (2) (v) – For Medical Informed Consent
42 CFR 482.43 (c) – For Discharge Planning Informed Consent

For facilities that are accredited by the Joint Commission (JC), they use another set of guidelines to promote safety for all involved. Every year the JC prints a manual outlining their standards and any changes that have been made from the year before.

Informed consent is in a section entitled Ethics, Rights and Responsibilities. The sections are further broken down into: Standards, Rationales, Elements of Performance, and Scoring (RI). Within the language of this section, JC makes more demands for compliance with informed consent. They are looking for specific information on the consent form that describes procedures, risks, benefits and interventions.

The authoritative sources make a strong case for getting their point across. The individual facilities then have the obligation to develop facility-specific policies.

In the above example, the clinic allowed the informed consent to remain in the chart and be valid for up to 5 days. The consent was not valid. The patient could become a plaintiff if she feels the procedure did not end in a fashion she was expecting. She is emotionally upset and having martial problems because of it. The disease is not her physician's fault; however, if the outcome fails to produce the effects expected, that could result in a lawsuit. The patient was also under mild sedation, so could not be asked to sign the consent. If the patient decided to sue, she might have a very strong case against this physician. Nurses have to make certain their documentation can hold up in court. Documenting the facts is a key to remaining on the outside of a lawsuit.

In the scenario that began this chapter, what should Stormie document? Her documentation needs to reflect the facts. She does not need to document anything about consent unless she witnessed the consent process. She does need to be aware that if the physician had asked her to wake the patient and assist with obtaining a witnessed consent, she could become part of a negligence claim. It is the circumstances surrounding the events that could be detrimental to the outcome. What was the final outcome to this story?

As Dr. Drigger was checking to make certain the repair was completed correctly, she looks up at Stormie with a relieved expression. Then she gives the thumbs up. She pulls down her mask and smiles, and wipes the imaginary sweat from her brow.

Mrs. Wargo is waking up. Her vital signs are stable and she is given a warm blanket.

Dr. Drigger gently takes her hand. "Mrs. Wargo, everything looks good. I'm glad you came in this morning. It turns out there was a tiny flap of skin that was missing an extra stitch. A very easy fix. I noticed that you have a lot of healthy tissue just waiting to heal. From the way things look, you should start to feel better very soon. As soon as you are ready, get dressed and meet me in my office, I'd like to answer any questions you might have."

Fifteen minutes later, Mrs. Wargo is sitting in Dr. Drigger's office. Stormie is asked to bring in the couple's counseling information along with a fresh informed consent form. All three of them sit down.

"Mrs. Wargo, as I mentioned to you, your surgical area looks very healthy. It will take a few days for you to feel like yourself again. Here is some information about what you can expect after this surgery.

"Just before the pre-procedural medication took effect," Dr. Drigger continues, "I realized that the consent form you signed for the first procedure had expired. Would you mind signing another one? The information I need to tell you is the same: the risks and benefits and what would happen if you did not have the procedure. I will be happy to go over any question you have. If you don't have any questions, could you sign on this line here and Stormie will sign as your witness and this paper will go into your chart."

Mrs. Wargo looks over at paper. Then to Dr. Drigger, "No, I don't have any questions, but I'd like a copy. If my incision does not heal soon, I'm going to have to take further action. My husband won't even look at me."

Mrs. Wargo signs the informed consent form and hands it to Stormie. "Stormie," Mrs. Wargo asks, "could you please make a copy of this for me?"

"Sure." Stormie takes the informed consent, signs as the witness and is about to leave.

"Stormie," calls Dr. Drigger, "could you please bring Mrs. Wargo the couple's counseling schedule and topics please? Thanks".

As Stormie leaves the room, she hears Mrs. Wargo talking.

"Dr. Drigger, I am so sorry I have been a difficult patient. I love my husband so much and I am so afraid of losing him. I felt like I have blamed you for this illness and you are only trying to help. Do you think counseling will help?"

Documentation Strategies: Keep It Simple. Silly (KISS)

Sometimes a nurse does not know what to chart until the event is over. In this situation, it would be better to document the events after the patient's procedure was completed. This way, Stormie could summarize the events without stating all the issues leading up to them.

"Informed Consent signed by pt. PT left the clinic without any complaints. Discharge teaching was done, please see discharge sheet. PT verbalized understanding to call our office... if she has any questions or concerns."

Resources:

O'Leary, K. et. al. (2010). Hospitalized patients' understanding of their plan of care. *Mayo Clinic Proceedings, 85*(1), 47-52. DOI: 10.4065\mcp.2009.0232.

Paterick, T. et al. (2008). Medical informed consent: General considerations for physicians. [Mayo Clinic Proceedings March 2008]. *Mayo Foundation for Medical Education and Research, 83*(3): 313-319. DOI: 10.4065/83.3.313.

Chapter 12
Nursing Student Rotation at Stream Home Healthcare

"Frank, what time did you get here?" His classmate, Jim Hightower, asked.

Frank Dunkin is waiting in the parking lot at Stream Home Healthcare Agency. He has been pretty excited about his imminent clinical experience. Frank has verbalized to everyone in his class that he knows this part of nursing like the back of his hand, and now that his class of nursing students is in their home care/clinic rotation, he views this as a chance to show what he can do. Everyone in his class knows that Frank's mother is a home care nurse; ever since Frank can remember, she took him along on home care visits. He feels very much at ease with this population.

Frank has gone so far as to brag about some of the things that he said his mother let him do when he was younger. For example, Frank said that he was allowed to mimic her with the clean and sterile dressing technique, he knows all about proper bag technique and he can even fill out the Oasis forms. He said that he could tell what a skilled nursing visit meant, even to the point of how some bills get denied because the nurse/ documenter didn't show a relationship between the patient, the provider and the insurance company. Frank even told Jim, another nursing student in his class, that even though today's clinical experience is to be spent as an observer, Frank was going to do the skills the nurse was assigned to do for the visit.

While Frank has attended nursing school, he's often annoyed others because of what he believes he already knows. Many of his fellow students didn't want to be around him because he was willing to take too many chances. He always wants to act like a full-fledged nurse and he has been known to challenge nurses in the past during clinical experiences. Someone in Frank's class heard that he failed a clinic rotation once because the instructor challenged Frank's safety standards. Of course, the rumor also had it that his mother saved him, and that Frank was allowed to repeat the class without the incident appearing on his permanent record.

Jim and Frank get out of their cars and are met by other students. They collectively make their way into the waiting room of the home care office and wait for their instructors and assignments.

Steve Beynor, RN, is a home care nurse at Stream Home Healthcare Agency. He usually enjoys the students and values the time he gets to spend with them. He and his wife, Janet, have an ongoing discussion about nursing students, as she's a nursing instructor in another county. Janet has often discussed with Steve the problems she's had with other nurses who are in clinical settings, stating that she wishes they would allow her to do her job. When she reports to the nursing director at West Brook Nursing School, she finds it difficult to give complete assessments of her students because she isn't personally able to assess their clinical skills. She also has expressed to Steve the trouble she's had giving her students the experiences that will best round out their skills.

Just last night, Janet talked with Steve about a student who was going behind her back by asking all the nurses on the unit to which he was assigned if there was anything he could do for them. She had told this student more than once that he is to shadow the nurse who is assigned to his patient; when there is a skill to be performed, he is to get the full-fledged nurse and they can do it together so the much more experienced nurse will be able to help Janet's student if he forgets to do anything.

Steve agrees with his wife that the nurse/supervisor needs to watch the nursing students closely, but believes that is not so much of a problem in home care. There's a one-to-one ratio (one nurse, one patient), and the students he's had with him usually know they're to use the home care clinical experience for observational purposes only.

At the last monthly meeting at Stream Home Healthcare, the nursing director spoke about the revised relationship between

Stream Home Healthcare and West Brook Nursing School. The meeting reiterated that all students are to observe the actions of the RN only, then write a paper about their experiences. The only time a student is allowed to touch a patient is after they have completed the agency documentation and been cleared with the agency, just like the employees.

There is a program at Stream that allows any nurse who wants to precept an opportunity to do so. All they must do is complete a ten-hour preceptor course, pass the test, then commit to one nursing student per semester. In exchange, the nurse will get a 10% hourly raise per semester. Almost all the nurses in the agency were willing to partake in this. Steve has been thinking about it, but hasn't yet made up his mind .

Steve comes into the office and notices the students gathered in the lobby. He isn't in the mood to deal with students today because he's behind on his documentation due to the quality time he and his wife spent last evening. He walks over to his cubicle and starts assembling his charts for the day. Then, as normal, Steve starts making his phone calls to let his patients know approximately what time they can expect him.

Steve has six patients today and he'll probably drive about seventy-five miles. One of his patients, Mr. Rosen with ALS, has been on Steve's census for about eight months. Like many home care nurses, Steve's routine is pretty stable and Mr. Rosen is completely used to it. Steve comes in, washes his hands, lays out his bag and supplies on the table near the bed. Next, he takes vital signs while asking questions about how Mr. Rosen's been feeling. Then, Steve does a dressing change, a Foley catheter change or perhaps a medication refill. Mr. Rosen lives with his daughter, who works during the day. She is unable to learn many of the skills that are required to care for her father without the support of daily home care visits. Many of Steve's patients end up on this sort of routine. Mr. Rosen enjoys the trust that has been established between himself and Steve, which is why Steve wouldn't want a nursing student to come between that.

While in Steve is in deep thought about the day, Frank approaches Steve's desk.

"Excuse me, are you Steve Beynor? I'm Frank Dunkin, the nursing student from West Brook Nursing School. I'm assigned to hang out with you today."

"Great. Have a seat; we'll leave in about fifteen minutes." While Steve's being quite polite about it all, Steve realizes that he is not in the mood for company. Steve gets up and leaves Frank standing at the cubicle's entrance. He walks into his manager's office and closes the door.

"May I have a word with you, Mattie? I really don't want to deal with a nursing student today. I thought we were going to be starting that next week. Please, I can't deal with him today."

"Sorry," Mattie replies, "but everyone else is booked and besides, he won't be any bother to you. He's smart and could be used as an assistant. You know, someone to tie your trash up or clean your supplies before placing them back in your bag. Just remember that he is not to touch the patients. You know what happened with that lawsuit that was in the paper the other day, where the patient sued the facility for battery."

When Steve gets back to his desk with the assignment he cannot amend, he glances over at Frank. Frank is showing his industry by creating care plans for all the patients on the list. *"Well,"* thinks Steve, *"maybe this novice will make a great assistant."*

Steve and Frank decide to drive down together. Steve figured that since Frank isn't going to be doing any "hands-on" in the patients' homes, their time in the car could be used as instructional time. Steve thought he could review each patient as they are driving, determine Frank's knowledge base, supplement where needed and, if they had time, they could stop off at a restaurant that has a nice bathroom and free WiFi. The agency does have a pretty nice electronic documentation system, but the WiFi isn't always dependable while driving. There have been times when Steve thought all his notes had been downloaded, but it hadn't happened. Steve likes to take a short lunch and download his notes during the day. He was already a little pressed from yesterday and really didn't have time to socialize with the student. He was willing to take Frank along, but things were going to progress as smoothly as possible so they could finish in time for Steve to pick his daughter up from school.

As soon as Frank gets into the car he asks "Which patients are you going to treat and which ones can I treat?"

"What?" says Steve.

"Who are the patients that you don't want to do? I'll take those."

"Frank, is that your name? I don't know anything about you and your clinical skill level. I'm sorry, but I can't let you touch any of my patients."

Frank starts laughing. One of those "you've gotta be kidding" laughs.

"Steve, man, I was told that I would be able to get some hands-on experience. Some actual home care nursing experience. Look, I know what I'm doing; please give me a chance to show you. I'll be wasting your time and mine if you don't let me do at least one thing out there in the field today. Please."

Steve looks down into his lap. He thinks for a split second that it wouldn't be that bad if this guy did a simple dressing change or pre-poured some medications with his strict supervision. *If I set up Mr. Rosen's meds,* he thinks to himself *and Frank puts them in the medication box, Frank wouldn't be touching the patients at all.* He turns to Franks and says. "We'll see".

Mr. Rosen was the third stop, and by this time, Steve and Frank have established a pretty simple routine. Steve tells Frank about the patient before they get to the patient's home, then they talk about the signs and symptoms to look for in the patient according to the medical diagnosis, family dynamics, prognosis, time since last hospitalization, insurance, and the health literacy of the patient and/or caregivers.

Health literacy is a huge variable, Steve explains. It really makes a significant difference in the amount of visits a person is entitled to. Since a significant part of the role of a home care nurse is that of a teacher, the nurse-as-teacher has to establish the literacy level of the person and work from that perspective. He goes on to explain that home care documentation relies very heavily on the nurse's ability to teach the patient or caregiver how to manage the patient's disease.

"Next stop is Mr. Rosen's," Frank says excitedly, "isn't that the medication container you said I could fill?"

"Frank, I've been thinking and I don't think it's a great idea for you to do anything outside of what the established relationship with my agency and your school has. I know that you are probably more than capable of filling the meds and you are probably very smart and conscientious about what you're doing, but I didn't make the rules and I don't feel comfortable allowing you to do that."

"Oh, please, Steve; I promise I won't do anything stupid, you can trust me."

"No, Frank. You see, I have to be an honest documenter. I have to document the care that I provide, not just what was done to – and for – my patient. I do trust you, but think about the whole nurse license exam. We take the NCLEX because the state wants to know that each professional is safe and can use prudent judgment independent of another person. My license or my insurance does not cover me in the event that something goes wrong while we we're working together.

"Just last week, we had a meeting about your school. The boss made it pretty clear that you are not to touch the patients or provide any of the skills. Pouring medication is a skill that only the professional nurse or the caregiver should be carrying out. Sorry, Frank; I can't let you do that."

"You are such a sissy, Steve. I can't believe you won't let me put a few pills in the medication box. What is the big deal? I've gone on hundreds of home visits with my mother and she usually lets me do some of the stuff she has to do. Then she'll ask me what I did and she documents. I've been doing this kind of stuff since I was about ten, and nothing bad has ever happened before.

"Look, if you don't let me help, I'm gonna go back and tell Mattie, your boss, that you broke sterile technique in that last patient's house. That patient also has a low grade temp and you didn't call the doctor or treat the condition with acetaminophen."

Steve looks at Frank long and hard. He cannot believe what this guy has just said. He cannot believe that Frank has threatened to make up a story and risk Steve's license and reputation because Frank's not allowed to do something that is not within the established policy of the relationship between the school and Stream, his employer. Steve is stunned that this student has been allowed to come this far in the nursing program and no one has realized that he is a danger to the community and nursing's reputation.

Steve now knows exactly what needs to be done. He is now well aware why he got stuck with Rosa Dunkin's son and how she must have used her power to get him this far. Doesn't she realize that he is a looney tune?

Do not say another word. Steve thinks, *just drive back to the Stream, drop him off and continue making my visits. Once he is out of my car, I'll call Mattie.*

"Frank, I just realized that I have to go back to the office and drop something off."

Steve goes back to the office and explains the events to Mattie. She thanks him for the information and the actions he took. She asks him to put everything in writing, using as many quotes as he could remember, and she assures him that she is going to speak with the nursing instructor, then the director of the school. Mattie felt this issue needed to be resolved quickly.

Steve feels relieved about reporting Frank. He knows that even nursing students can get sued. Steve might have saved this young man a world of trouble in the future. Just as crucial is the potential unsafe care patients could have received. Now Steve can get back to patient care. *"Oh",* he thinks, *"I better call those last three patients and tell them I am running a little behind schedule."*

Chapter 13
Small Hospital, Large Dilemmas

Youth General is a hospital in suburban America. Doctor Amy Hest-Bander has been an Orthopedic attending there ever since she completed her fellowship. Dr. Andrew Hest, Sr., is her father and an original member of the hospital's board of directors.

Dr. Hest-Bander has a reputation of being easygoing and relatively approachable. She has two young children with her husband, Cory Bander, who is a nursing supervisor at the same hospital. Normally, their relationship does not interfere with the mechanics of patient care. But there are times you can tell there is trouble in paradise. The staff was aware of the ebbs and flows of their relationship, but it never really made an impact in patient care decisions until one time in January.

"What's today's date?" Dr. Hest-Bander asked anyone in earshot of the question at the nurses station.

"It's the 21st!" yells Harry Pina, RN.

As Dr. Hest-Bander finishes writing her notes and orders, she asks another general question. "Who is taking care of my new patient, Robert Appel, with the right ankle fracture in 411?"

"I am," replies Nurse Pina, "Why?"

"I've written orders for Mr. Appel to be seen by Nephrology; we did a closed reduction while he was in the ED and I am admitting him under guarded condition because of his history of poor peripheral circulation. I believe he is a patient of Dr. Ethan Barnett. Thanks."

As Dr. Hest-Bander closes the chart and quickly walks away, Nurse Pina is left with his mouth open. "Boy, she didn't give me a chance to finish. I was going to tell her that Dr. Barnett is out of town and Dr. Baylor is covering for him. I guess that doesn't really matter anyway."

Nurse Pina organizes his report sheet, checks all his orders, then leaves the nurses station to begin his rounds. He uses a report sheet that he designed. It has all the vital patient information on it with symbols and codes that he made up himself. He also has a timeline along the side of each patient's information. He finds this helpful, especially on busy days when many things seem to happen all at once. He feels that being a firefighter in addition to being a nurse has helped him be more organized and respectful of his time and his patients.

One of Nurse Pina's good friends was found guilty in a nursing malpractice lawsuit because she couldn't prove in her documentation exactly when she went to check on a patient. The patient was without pulse and respirations when she went in there, but she stated she had been in to check the patient just five minutes earlier. The patient did not survive the code. Her license was suspended for three years. Ever since then, every time Nurse Pina makes improvements to his report sheet, he makes certain there is a timeline included.

Nurse Pina has worked as an orthopedic nurse for many years. He spends his off shifts working for the town's volunteer fire department. He is one of those nurses with the confidence of two people. His head is always held high, he is always available to help if needed, and he is a whiz at the computer.

As he completes his assessment of Mr. Appel, the patient complains of discomfort to his right ankle at the fracture site. As Nurse Pina is palpating for pain, swelling, temperature and odor, Mr. Appel grabs his hand. "Oh, that really hurts! Please don't touch my ankle."

"I'm sorry, Mr. Appel, but since I cannot see underneath that bandage, I have to do as many things as possible to determine if you are healing properly."

"I realize that, but that really hurts. Can I get something for the pain?"

"Sure," replies Nurse Pina. "On a scale of one to ten, with ten being the worst pain you've ever felt, can you tell me how you would rate your pain?"

"It's a seven," Mr. Appel says, "and it's constant and throbbing."

Nurse Pina goes back to the chart to review the pain medication orders, check for allergies and any dressing orders and then checks the MAR. He notices there are no orders to remove the dressing but he can give the patient either Acetaminophen or Oxycodone. He decides on the Oxycodone.

When he goes back into the room and administers the medication, he puts his nose as close as possible to the soft bandage. There is a foul odor, he thinks. He's not certain and decides that he will re-check this towards the end of his shift.

Later on when Nurse Pina is writing some notes, he looks through Mr. Appel's chart. He notices that in addition to the patient being on dialysis, he also has PVD. "Oh, that's right;" he thinks to himself, " *Dr. Hest-Bander mentioned that as the reason he was admitted, so why didn't she write dressing orders?"*

Nurse Pina calls Dr. Baylor, the Nephrologist, as ordered. Dr. Baylor is familiar with Mr. Appel. He tells Nurse Pina that he will be there in the morning to check on him and if there are any concerns with the patient from a nephrology perspective, please do not hesitate to call again. He thanks Nurse Pina for the call and hangs up.

Nurse Pina did not work as a volunteer firefighter last evening, but he did get a call from one of his buddies at the firehouse that morning telling him about a call they responded to at the Hest-Bander home the night before. The details were a little sketchy, but apparently the smoke detector which is wired to the security system had been activated.

When the fire department arrived, Dr. Hest-Bander refused to let the firefighters in. She said everything was under control. But as his buddy told him, there was a suspicious odor coming from inside the house. The etiology was very difficult to identify.

"What the heck do you think was going on in there?" Asked Nurse Pina.

"I don't know," replied his friend, "but there is definably something going on."

Toward the end of the shift, Nurse Pina goes back to make a last check on Mr. Appel. The patient complains again of constant and throbbing pain to his ankle. "Please do something," Mr. Appel begs. "I don't think I can take this pain any longer."

"Okay," replies Nurse Pina, "But please understand that I have called Dr. Hest-Bander several times; I am waiting for her to call back. Please be patient. I will call the nursing supervisor next and keep you informed as to what is going on."

Nurse Pina rushes back to the nurse's station and pages the nursing supervisor, Cory Bander. Finally the operator calls Nurse Pina back to report that Nurse Bander has stepped out of the building for a few moments and should be back shortly.

"A few moments? I have been trying to reach him for forty minutes! I have an impending emergency on my hands and I cannot seem to reach anyone!"

He hangs up and calls Dr. Baylor. "Dr. Baylor, I am sorry to bother you, but I have a problem with Mr. Appel. He is complaining of severe pain to his right ankle. I've given all the meds that are ordered and I am unable to reach Dr. Hest-Bander or anyone else from the Ortho service, and I am smelling something unusual from his ankle and do not have any orders to remove the dressing. Can you please advice me?"

"Certainly," replies Dr. Baylor. "I'm in the house right now. I'll be there in about five minutes."

When Nurse Pina hangs up, he wonders if the call to the fire department last evening has anything to do with the course of events that have taken place today. He writes his notes very carefully, making certain to acknowledge a timeline that will demonstrate his prudent judgment and timely attempts to contact the attending physician and nursing supervisor.

When Dr. Baylor arrives fifteen minutes later, Nurse Pina immediately takes him to Mr. Appel's room. They find Mr. Appel diaphoretic, tachypnic, febrile and rating his pain ten out of ten. Dr. Baylor orders the dressing to be removed immediately. Once it's gone, they find the patient's skin to be mottled, macerated and cool to the touch. Neither the nurse or the doctor were able to assess a digital pedal pulse, but once the Doppler was placed, they found a faint pedal pulse.

Several days later, Mr. Appel underwent a right above-the-knee amputation. He was a professional ice hockey coach.

Being an amputee will make it very difficult to earn a living as an ice hockey coach. His salary went from seven figures down to nothing.

Regardless of the state in which you live, there are rules and regulations for nurses. As licensed professionals, we are governed in our actions by both state and federal laws. These laws are written with various phrases and divided into various categories of practice settings and scenarios, but the message is the same.

Nurses are licensed in the signs and symptoms of illness or disease. We are the "A" team: the assessment team. We spend countless hours in the study of disease manifestations and the symptoms of diseases. We are well aware of the assessment criteria we gather, whether it is through our senses, the lab report, a patient report and a handing off report. We are to observe what we find in the patient and report any abnormalities to the appropriate person for further management if needed. But there are so many times when the situation comes with extra baggage. In fact, it usually does.

Lawsuits can occur when a patient has a bad outcome, even if the nursing staff has done all of the right things. But what happens if the decisions made are based on the wrong things?

In the example above, we have a family that is enmeshed with the facility. Dr. Hest-Bander's father is a senior member of the hospital staff and he is on the Board of Directors. Her husband is a nursing supervisor. Their relationship at the hospital is not usually affected by their personal challenges, until perhaps this time. Although this story could be viewed as an extreme circumstance, there are many times when personal experiences play a role in decision-making.

Nurse Pina is a very confident, self-assured nurse who keeps the relationships of his colleagues outside of his nursing judgment. It is not always easy to do this. There are nurses who would fear disciplinary actions for insubordination if they express their opinions about a senior member of a facility.

"Whistleblowing" is making headlines and nurses are gaining momentum in the battle against healthcare providers who do not adhere to the standards of care. But we have a very long road ahead.

There was a case involving a young man who came in for one-day surgery and after a series of missed opportunities to notify a doctor, the patient died. The nurses testified that the attending had implied that he was not to be called unless all the orders written had been exhausted. They feared calling him because he had a reputation of being rude, sarcastic and condescending. They had complained several times to nursing management about his constant comments of belittlement and degradation, but administration did not support their position. Nurse Pina spoke with Dr. Hest-Bander at the beginning of the shift. He could have been put off by her quick attempt to report off her orders and concern for the patient's admission. She stated, "I am admitting him under guarded condition because of his history of peripheral vascular disease." He recalls this as he is assessing the patient's severe discomfort and the suspicious odor coming from the dressing site.

After receiving the call from his fellow firefighter friend, Nurse Pina could have had trepidation over calling Dr. Hest-Bander. But that does not stop him. He calls her several times, not thinking twice about the personal problems she might be experiencing. He does not use the information from last night's events to determine what actions to take on behalf of his patient.

Our license states that when there is a deviation from the baseline assessment, a physician or designee needs to be notified for further interventions. It doesn't state how soon the medical professional needs to be called, but the use of prudent nursing judgment comes into question; the sooner, the better. After several attempts to reach the doctor, Nurse Pina decides to contact someone following the chain of command and calls his nursing supervisor. After waiting forty minutes, he was still unable to reach Dr. Hest-Bander or Nurse Bander, so he calls Dr. Baylor, the nephrologist.

When faced with a situation like this, it is crucial to document your findings, actions, communication attempts or lack thereof on a timeline. Documenting in quotes is very helpful with regards to your defense.

You want to be able to prove that you did everything within your professional scope of practice to keep the patient safe and the situation in control. It is often your narrative notes that provide a summary for the events. Take good notes and document, document, document. Sometimes you have to over-document to make certain points clear, while other times, less is more. Routinely summarizing your information is a strong defense.

Here is one way the narrative notes might be written.

9:30 am - Patient c/o pain to right ankle, states "that really hurts, please don't touch my ankle." Pain rated as 7/10. Medicated with Oxycodone. See MAR and V/S

10:30 am - Pain now 5/10. Medicated with Acetaminophen. See MAR. Telephone call to Dr. Baylor (000) 555-1212. He stated he will visit the patient tomorrow.

10:30 am - Questionable foul odor from right ankle. Will re-assess.

12:30 pm - Patient c/o pain "Constant and throbbing" 7/10. Medicated with Oxycodone. See MAR. Re-assessed odor. Mild foul.

1:30 pm - Pt c/o pain 6/10 medicated with Acetaminophen. See MAR and V/S. Repositioned for comfort. Family at the bedside.

3 pm - Patient resting with eyes closed. RR 16. Used hospitals nonverbal pain scale.

5 pm – Patient complaining of pain. Medicated, see MAR. Call

placed to Dr. Hest-Bander (000) 555-1234, awaiting call back. Message left on voice mail, all information on MAR and pain scale left in message.

5:46 pm - Patient is still complaining of "Constant and throbbing pain", 9/10 asking that something be done. I explained that I am waiting for Dr. Hest-Bander to call me back. And that I will call the nursing supervisor and let him know as soon as I hear from someone.

6:05 pm - Call placed to (000) 555-1234 Dr. Hest-Bander and Nursing Supervisor called (000) 555-1226 and are overhead paged.

6:15 pm - Call placed to (000) 555-1234 Dr. Hest-Bander

6:25 pm - Overhead paged Dr. Hest-Bander and Nurse Cory Bander

6:30 pm - Call from the page operator, Elizabeth Porter, she states Nurse Cory Bander stated he was stepping out for a moment and should return shortly.

6:31 pm - Called Dr. Baylor and spoke with him, he states he will come and see the patient immediately.

6:50 pm - Dr. Baylor present, gave orders to remove dressing, clean and re-dress. See MD orders. Skin is macerated, mottled, unable to obtain pulse with manual palpation, Doppler required. Neurological assessment done, see neuro assessment. See V/S and physical assessment for details.

These notes help to defend or justify that the nurse was making timely assessments, made several attempts to notify the attending, then the nursing supervisor and ultimately another physician.

As you travel through your shift caring for patients, take

notes along a timeline chronology. At the end of your shift, you can determine what information is important regarding the outcome of the patient. If nothing happens to a patient during your shift, then the details that you have been documenting on your report sheet can be shredded without a re-write. But there is a chance that you will need to hold yourself accountable for the "what ifs." "If" is during those instances when having times and details are utilized in your favor. If you have a photographic (eidetic) memory, then use your memory to create a picture that tells the story.

Most people are not able to recall specific details on several things going on at the same time. Write down events as they happen as best as you can. Create a code sheet or a shorthand for yourself, then decide for yourself at the end of the shift if your information translates into prudent nursing judgment. Documentation is telling a story and that is how attorneys conceptualize the events.

Suppose Nurse Pina had been relaxed about his documentation. Dr. Hest-Bander and Nurse Cory Bander would have an easier time telling a jury that they did not receive an overhead page or cell phone calls. Nurse Pina wrote down the name of the hospital operator and proof that he had been trying to reach the nurse and doctor for at least forty minutes. These are factors that add weight in your favor.

The goal of documenting with legal standards means taking the standards of nursing as we know them and creating a document demonstrating that we did what is within that scope. Time lines are key to that delivery.

Chapter 14
Mr. Janisker goes to the ED

Before Evan Janisker went to the emergency room, he knew he should have gone sooner. His skin looked sallow and the dark circles around his eyes were getting darker. He had difficulty getting up in the morning even though he used to have a lot of energy. Lately, he thought there was blood in his stool, but wasn't certain. He often would stop at the neighborhood bar for a couple of drinks before heading home. He knew drinking alcohol was frowned upon by his doctor because of all the ulcers they'd found in his stomach, his history of heavy drinking, and some liver damage. But since his wife left and took the kids, he took less time to care for himself. He wasn't watching for the worsening stomach symptoms his doctor had told him about nor eating the foods the dietitian had recommended. He thought perhaps that he was depressed, and planned to get pills for depression at the emergency department because lately life seemed more and more unbearable.

Evan signs in at the ED registration desk and waits to be called. At this small rural hospital, the patients who walk in are initially screened and registered before seeing a nurse. Many patients have been using this facility as a clinic and administration feels the best use of staff is to have pre-screening and registration done first when the patients walk in.

Bruce, the young man in hospital scrubs, is a Patient Care Technician (PCT). Evan thought that the man smelled like a bottle of cheap cologne and wondered if he made a mistake coming to the hospital. He doesn't want to be in the hospital, but knows that his condition is becoming serious. His vision fades and he finds it hard to concentrate. He really believes he needs depression medicine to get back to the person he used to be.

"So, Mr. Janisker, what brings you in today?" Bruce asks.

"Well, I have not been feeling like myself lately. I am tired all the time. I don't have much of an appetite and I don't seem to be able to concentrate at work." He pauses, then adds, "I think I need pills for depression."

"Oh," says Bruce. As the PCT is obtaining vital signs and a brief history, he asks Evan, "What kind of work do you do?"

"I design and build stone walls," Evan answers with pride. "Do you know the Jenkins building up on 3rd and Main Street, you know, downtown near the entrance to the park? Well, I built that one."

"You built that one? It's nice," says Bruce

"Yeah, thanks," Evan says. He begins to feel proud and worthy for a moment and forgets that he doesn't feel well. It is these moments of elation that have caused the delay in his treatment. Over the past few months he has used alcohol and social banter to ward off his symptoms.

"Mr. Janisker, do you take any medication?" asks Bruce

"No," Evan replies.

Bruce's notes upon Evan's admission

Vital signs - 100/59, 90, 22, 99T.
Items Checked:
Skin - wet and cool to the touch.
Eyes – WNL, Comments – shifting a lot, nervous
Behavior – fidgety, not staying focused.
Not in acute distress.
CC: "I think I am depressed."
Patient states that he has poor appetite, poor sleeping, not focused, not feeling rested in the morning.

The PCT reviews the collected information. He doesn't usually work in the ED and this is only the third time he's floated here. He wants to make the right choices and wonders if the vital signs are something to be alarmed about. He remembers the last time he alerted the ED triage nurse to vital signs that he thought where out of range and they weren't. The nurse was so mad that he made a big deal about it; she made him feel really awful and he swore that he would never make that mistake again. So he decides that these vital signs are still within the normal range and does not say anything to the triage nurse.

He convinces himself that the patient came in for depression because that's what the patient said was wrong with him. He makes the decision to have him register with Melissa, the admitting clerk, before going to the triage nurse.

Just before Bruce takes the patient over to Melissa's area, Evan remembers the medication list he keeps in his wallet. "Oh, here is a copy of the medication I am taking," says Mr. Janisker. The PCT takes the list and looks it over. The PCT thinks that maybe there is something to be concerned about with this guy since he just said he doesn't take any medications.

"Do you know what all these pills are for?" Bruce asks.

"Yes." Evan stops, thinks hard, then goes on. "Norvac – it's for my heart and blood pressure, I think. Colace helps me go to the bathroom. Aspirin – I think I'm to take this so I won't have a stroke. Prevacid is for my stomach – I guess my job has stressed me out over the past few years, and sometimes I feel like there is a hole in my stomach."

As Bruce is writing all this down, Evan goes on with, "I know that I am not to eat a lot of spicy foods or drink alcohol, but you know those are sometimes the best combinations." Evan looks up at Bruce with a nod and a wink. "Nurse, are you married?"

The PCT notices the patient called him "nurse", but does not correct him. He's flattered that the gentleman believes he is a nurse. He thinks about all the people who have commented about the way he manages patients and how he is always being mistaken as a nurse. He wonders if he should really pursue nursing school.

"Nah," says Bruce, "I'm only 22."

"Well, women can really mess you up. My wife of fifteen years walked out on me. She took our kids said, she needed to get away from me; I was causing her too much misery. She said I flirted with every female I meet. She told me that I needed to grow up. I haven't seen my kids in months."

Evan pauses again, then goes on more firmly. "I'm here because I'm a depressed man. I really feel so sad about all the things that have happened over the last few months."

Okay, thinks Bruce, *this guy is an emotional wreck.*

"I started feeling this way since they left," Evan adds. "My heart is broken."

Bruce continues to listen to the patient.

Evan goes on with, "I'm probably just a little depressed, but I always thought that depression was for people who are weak in the mind. Sometimes I think I see blood in my stool, but I'm not sure. I really haven't cared much since my family walked out on me."

As the PCT puts his head down to write all of the complaints of the patient, Evan Janisker closes his eyes in exhaustion. *"I am so tired,* he says to himself, *"I could fall asleep right now."* Evan looks up at Bruce and realizes that this young man looks about 18 years old. "You're not really a nurse, are you?"

"No," Bruce admits. "I am a patient care technician."

"Oh, why didn't you say so in the first place?" Evan asks.

Evan feels like he is wasting his time in the ED. He's never really sick and doesn't trust the healthcare system anyway. He feels like all people do is ask questions about health insurance before they want to treat you. His wife used to handle all this stuff.

He's thinking about walking out again. Maybe call his medical doctor in the morning and make an appointment. But he feels awful and needs to stay.

Bruce excuses himself for a moment.

Evan puts his head down and cries. *"What has happened to my life? I am falling apart and there is no one here to help me."* He pulls himself together just as Bruce comes back with an attractive young lady.

"Are you Evan Janisker?"

Bruce introduces Melissa, the clerk, to Evan. Evan perks up. *"Well,"* he thinks to himself, *"this is the kind of hospital employee that I can appreciate."*

"Hi, my name is Melissa; can you please follow me?

I have to get some information from you before the nurse can see you."

"Sure," Evan says aloud. Inside, he thought, "*I'll follow you anywhere.*"

As they round the corner, Evan forgets his symptoms. As Melissa went down the column of questions, the two exchanged subtle glances.

They are sitting across from each other and, as Melissa shuffles the papers around, there is an awkward silence. Melissa, a woman who looks older than her 29 years, has a nervous way of kicking her crossed leg. Several times during the exchange, she kicked Evan. They both thought it was funny.

"So, Mr. Janisker, do have your insurance card with you?"

"Oh," Evan says. "Is that all you people care about? Yes, I have my card; do you care why I came in here?"

"Yes, I do," Melissa says.

"I have been more and more tired," Evan says. "Sometimes, when I use the bathroom, I think I see blood in the toilet, but most of the lights in my bathroom need to be changed and I haven't had the energy to change the bulbs. My wife left me not too long ago and the truth is I have been feeling like crap."

"Oh," replies Melissa, "Now may I see your card?" She processes his paper work.

Evan is feeling a wave of light-headedness again, but won't admit it. He's upset over the bureaucracy at the hospital and again feels like going home. His vision is blurry and he is pretending that he can read and sign the forms.

Melissa giggles and so does Evan. He tries to relax. She continues to ask him a series of questions. As she looks up for the last time before completing the registration process she notices that he is perspiring; Evan's skin has a glistening layer of moisture. She hands him a tissue and he wipes the sweat from his brow.

"Mr. Janisker, could you please hold out your hand? I'd like to put this band around your wrist." She does so, then says, "Now you are officially our patient. Let's hurry up and get you over to the nurse. Do you need a wheelchair?"

"Heck no, I'm as strong as an ox!" replies Evan.

Melissa looks over her work and leads him to the triage area.

Janet Smith, RN, is a slightly stocky woman raising three kids alone. Nurse Smith walks with a slight limp that is more exaggerated since this is her fifth straight 12-hour shift. She had been about to go on her break when Melissa walks up to her station. *"Oh brother,"* thought Nurse Smith, *"this could take a while."*

Melissa met her eyes. "Nurse Smith, this is Mr. Janisker. Here is his paperwork." Melissa and Evan exchange a lasting glance.

Nurse Smith could tell that Melissa was up to it again, always making goo-goo eyes with the patients. But she pushed that to the side. "Good evening, Mr. Janisker, my name is Janet Smith. I'll be your nurse here in triage. Please have a seat up on this table; I can help you, if you'd like."

"No, I can do it myself," Evan replies. As he is hoisting himself up to the table, he is unsteady and almost falls back.

Nurse Smith catches him; now she realizes that Evan is not feeling as well as he first appears.

Nurse Smith thinks back to the in-service she attended called *Injury By Falls, What Direct Healthcare Providers Need to Know.* The instructor told the class that falls are the leading cause of hospital injuries, and while they are on the list of most frequently reported sentinel events, falls can lead to serious injuries and sometimes death. The instructor told the class about a lawsuit in Georgia where an eighty-four-year-old woman was being transferred from her bed to a stretcher and, during the transfer, the patient was dropped and suffered bilateral fractures. The damage award went to the plaintiff for $250,000. The instructor went on to explain that, although the monetary award was minimal compared to other fall and injury cases in malpractice, these incidences, if they are reported to the state licensing board, stay on our licenses for quite some time.

Even though Nurse Smith graduated over fifteen years ago, she appreciates the in-services she attends. She tells the younger, less experienced nurses that it is very important to maintain current knowledge of general nursing and healthcare practices and to be especially careful about keeping up to date within the clinical area that they are practicing in. She feels the in-services help her stay current with today's changing healthcare climate.

Nurse Smith recalls the instructor talking about incident reports and how important it is to always tell the truth and to be factual in the documentation because it could be used in a lawsuit. The in-service instructor mentioned how nurses have never really been formally trained in writing incident reports. They often learn from another nurse who happens to be close by and has the time to assist with the process. The helping nurse might not know what happens to the report once it's generated.

Since that class, she realized now that forms follow a predicable pattern because they are merely internal tracking tools used to gather data to determine if changes in policy or people need to be made. The chart first goes to the charge nurse, then to the risk management department. The risk management department or a department with risk management responsibilities keeps track of all the incidences. (Medicalegal Concepts, 2010). They are really interested in keeping the facility safe, looking at trends and making changes in policy if some need to be made.

Incident reports also track employees. If they see a negative trend with an employee, they can either discipline the employee in question or release him of his duties.

The in-service instructor explained that there is a process in a nursing malpractice lawsuit called "discovery." It is during this time when many of the documents from the facility are gathered. The incident report could be one of those pieces of paper that the plaintiff's attorney could use to strengthen their case against a nurse.

Evan is now stabilized on the table and Nurse Smith has a chance to look over the chart. She sits down near the patient.

"Your blood pressure was 100/59 about 30 minutes ago. Do you know what your normal blood pressure is?"

"No, but the doctor has me on medication for it," Evan replies.

"Well that might be part of your problem; your blood pressure is on the low side, did you take your blood pressure medicine today?"

"Yes, I think so."

"I'll check your vital signs again," Nurse Evans said. "I see that you are also taking Prevacid and aspirin. Did your doctor tell you to take aspirin?"

"No, a friend of mine told me it stops stroke, so I started taking it about three months ago," Evan said.

Nurse Smith notices that the PCT noted that the patient c/o blood in his stool.

"Are you having blood in your stool?"

Evan ignores the question.

After a minute, Nurse Smith goes on. "What were the symptoms of your ulcer?"

"I had pain and burning in my stomach," Evan answers readily. "It was during the time that I was under a lot of stress at work."

"So, you're having blood in your stool?" Nurse Smith asks again.

"I don't have blood in my stool. I'm here because I've been feeling depressed since my wife left and took my kids with her. She complained that I talk to too many women and she cannot take it anymore."

"Okay, so you're here because you believe you're depressed?" Nurse Smith asks.

"I think I'm depressed," Evan says. "I can't get enough sleep. I'm tired all the time. Look at me. Is everyone here crazy? Could someone help me instead of asking me questions all the time? I need to see a doctor."

"Let me take another set of vital signs," Nurse Smith says. 90/55, 100, 24, 99.

"Mr. Janisker, have you noticed any blood in your stool?" Nurse Smith asks a third time.

"No, I told you. NO!"

"Okay." Nurse Smith does not waste anymore time. This patient might think he is here for depression, but she knows that is not his only problem. Nurse Smith picks up the phone to call the ED nursing station, and keeps her eyes on the patient.

"Hello, Mary, it's Janet, up in triage," she says. "I've got a patient here who I believe is going into shock with a possible GI bleed, but I'm no doctor and don't give a medical diagnosis. But from a nursing prospective, this guy is in trouble. Could you ask Dr. Rafety or whoever is available to come up here STAT? Thanks."

As soon as she hangs up the phone, it rings. "Janet, it's Mary. Dr. Rafety says initiate the shock protocol."

Janet says, "I've already done it all. I used the standing orders that are here."

We rely on our colleagues and patients to supply us with information that helps guide the care we administer. We are taught to gather information based on the patient's signs and symptoms, what we learn in nursing school and what the patient tells us. But often times the patients make it very difficult. We are then faced with the dilemma of an impending lawsuit, even when we have tried to follow all the protocols that we know.

When Mr. Jankister comes in to the hospital, he feels comfortable speaking openly to the first two people he interacts with. The information he shared with the PCT was documented on his chart. It was not reported to the triage RN. But Nurse Smith made a point to review the documents and interview the patient.

There are many ways to effectively communicate the care provided during a shift. In order to practice nursing in a way that keeps your license blemish-free, you must be serious and conscientious about your nursing systems with systems devised to meet your professional needs. Noisy nursing stations, frequent interruptions and a million other things going through our minds can take away the ability to properly chart what is going on. Lawsuits spring up everyday because of poor communication.

"Handing off" or the report process that occurs within the healthcare environment is crucial to the process of continuous care. We often think that the information written in the chart serves as an adequate communication tool or that a verbal report can satisfy all that is needed to continue providing care that is within the standards of practice. Often times it does not. Joint Commission has made the process of communication a major safety goal. They have termed the phrase "Handing Off" (Joint Commission, 2009) as the process where one healthcare provider is giving and/or receiving a report from another.

Lack of communication is the number one reason sentinel events occur. Sentinel events and lawsuits are closely tied. Just think: the standards of practice that a lawyer uses are the same standards used by the authoritative sources. As a medical or nursing malpractice case ensues, the plaintiff team will look for policies and procedures that will help support the allegations. The attorneys look for clinical practice articles to support the allegations of negligence. Joint Commission's statements are based on safety in the healthcare communities and lawyers like to know what the safety expectations are.

Nurse Smith was very accurate with her assessments and interventions. She had the experience to know that Evan Janisker's symptoms were more serious than Evan thought they were. Sometimes we place a high value on prior knowledge. We are expected to know what is wrong or right and this might be as a result of experiences gone south. But using critical thinking skills can only help those with experience. Understanding the fundamental rules, regulations and expectations of the nurse delivering care in the healthcare system will save the stress of an impending lawsuit with the nurse as the defendant.

The concept of "Handing Off" is designed to standardize the process of communication within a facility. There are guidelines that are to be addressed and carried out in a fashion that suits the end users. Handing Off protocols should be used whenever your patient is leaving your care, or you are receiving a patient. Include in your documentation the following information:

> Date and time of transfer
> Patient's condition (V/S)
> Who provided the transfer?
> Where/to whom the patient was transferred
> Manner of transfer

It would be beneficial to include all of these items (that are found on SBAR forms); however, with the ever-growing time constraints, you need to use your best nursing judgment to determine what would constitute a safe amount of defensible information. Realize that some information is better than none, and all is better than some.

Patient's Diagnosis or Diagnoses

Since effective communication implies open dialogue, it would be helpful to practice effective handing off procedures to include the patient/resident or client's diagnoses. Patient's have so many more co-morbidities than ever before and determining which ones to omit, if need be, comes down to the signs and symptoms and reason for the patient's admission, the medication they are on and the urgency of these issues. Although this might sound elementary, please understand it is these very behaviors in nursing that we take for granted that turn into the malpractice cases that we would like to avoid.

Recent Changes in Condition or Treatment

What are/is the primary reason for the person to be under your care? What test/procedures have taken place during their infirmity? What has occurred during your time with them before the hand-off? An interesting facet about medical or nursing malpractice is that, many times, there are tiny and virtual subtle changes in a patient's presentation that, when reviewed in a cumulative fashion demonstrate that the nurse might not have been paying attention. Think about the subtle changes in your patient's condition. Keep track of all the information you gather to determine if there are values that need to be passed on to the next care provider. The concept of a timeline chronology cannot be over exaggerated. Nurses need to be aware of the qualitative and quantitative information gathered during the shift.

Anticipated changes in condition or treatment

If you are aware of any upcoming tests or procedures for this client, please include that in your reporting process. As nurses, we have the opportunity to make the client's experience less stressful. As nurses, we schedule our tasks according to our shifts. Sure, we are making certain that our patients have their meds on time, or that they are prepped for examinations in a timely fashion. We are aware of the expectations that other healthcare providers place on us because they are looking to keep their schedule on task and we can appreciate that.

But what about our patients? Our patients would benefit from knowing what to expect during a shift or a stay at a facility.

I remember working on an orthopedic unit. It was during that experience when I found value in the concept of scheduling. While working with the orthopedic in-patient population, and even as a home care nurse whose facility was associated with an orthopedic institute, I learned that being aware of therapist schedules made the lives of my patients that much more consoling.

So how did that work? At the beginning of my shift, I would review my patients who were scheduled for therapy that day. Therapists are a lot like dentists. They have a list of patients scheduled for the day and they have a pretty good idea how long each of those visits is going to take. (CMS allocates their visit timeframe based on the diagnosis, complications and progress notes. They bill in units of fifteen- or twenty-minute intervals.) Therapists begin their day knowing the order in which they will visit their patients in addition to knowing the timeframe for the therapy session.

With this information, I was able to medicate my patients and get them dressed and ready so, when the therapist arrived, the patient was mentally and physically available for him or her. It is an awful situation when your patient misses therapy because he or she was not ready for the session and the therapist might not have time to come back that day.

If you are able to put some control in your day and bring a calming effect to your patients, why wouldn't you? This is part of the handing off process. Knowing what your patient can expect helps you know what to expect as well.

This concept is a perfect segue into the next requirement for a smooth hand-off. What can your patient expect in the next interval of care? If the nurse continues to follow patterns of progress or regress in the patient, it makes it easier to give an effective hand-off. If the nurse could have an account of the tests and basic results of the patient's process, that could facilitate the system.

Lawsuits happen when healthcare providers fail to communicate what is important. We know what is important, but we often fail to communicate it. Our fast-paced hand-off process has caused us to sometimes give and get reports on the telephone or via a taping session. If this is the pattern adopted by your facility, there needs to be timely consideration for questions and responses to take place.

When healthcare team members neglect to communicate essential facts, it could lead to injury to the patient or the staff. Practice defensive nursing by communicating significant facts about patient findings, reports or observations. Document conversations and keep a timeline for all that you do during each shift. Sometimes you might think something isn't important, but you never know. And so what if you give someone information they think is unessential? It is not for them to decide; for all they know, it could be a lawsuit saver.

Let's go back to Nurse Smith and Mr. Janisker. When the patient meets the nurse, he is exhausted mentally and physically. He doesn't understand the healthcare system. He didn't want to go to the hospital in the first place and finds the process humiliating. He wonders why he has to keep explaining the situation to everyone, and no one who really matters. So by the time he reaches the care of Nurse Smith, he doesn't feel like explaining his symptoms and is convinced that he's just depressed. This is not an uncommon feeling among patients. Patients really don't understand that information doesn't always get passed from one healthcare provider to another. They don't know that each unit has a different set of paperwork to complete, even if the information seems to overlap or repeat itself. When we meet Nurse Smith, we learn that she is a single mother. She has a limp that gets exacerbated when she is tired or after a long stretch of days on-shift. This is her 5th straight 12-hour shift. Since the average age of a nurse in 2011 is 48.8 years, physical strains on the job are not uncommon. Nurse Smith was getting ready to go on her break when in walk Mr. Janisker and Melissa.

What do her age and demographics have to do with a lawsuit? Medical malpractice attorneys want to build a strong case by looking all the facts that could communicate to a jury that a nurse made a bad judgment because of the surrounding circumstances. They are looking to find the deviation in the standard of care.

The paperwork received was completed by a Patient Care Technician. PCTs are unlicensed assistive personnel who possess a fraction of the knowledge of a nurse. They are Certified Nursing Assistants who have additional course work in communications, phlebotomy, healthcare privacy, infection control and medical safety. They are required to have some clerical skills as well. They are not versed in recognizing the signs and symptoms of disease or the interventions necessary to keep patients safe. They are trained either through a vocational college or technical school for one to two years, and work under the supervision of a nurse.

So when Bruce, our PCT, obtains vital signs from Mr. Janisker, he independently makes the decision to interpret them. That is outside his scope of practice. Here is questionable data, not poor past experiences. One situation should not negatively affect another. He thinks about another time when he reported vital signs and was chastised for doing so. Because of that past experience, he decided not to report Mr. Janisker's signs. People in healthcare are human and Bruce's past experience and poor judgment could have caused Mr. Janisker his life. Be aware of the people you are working around. Nursing can have a domino effect.

Poor communication dynamics in any situation can set the scene for disaster. But because Nurse Smith is familiar with triaging patients, she knows that using all of her clinical skills will allow her patient's problems to surface quickly. She is able to determine a discrepancy between his chief complaints, the documentation and her assessment. Using all of her senses, she provides quick and appropriate interventions that will save his life. There will be no lawsuit for Nurse Smith or this facility. This could be considered a "near-miss."

Resources:

Rosseter, R.J. (2010). Nursing shortage fact sheet. *American Association of Colleges of Nursing.* Accessed March 23, 2010 http://www.aacn.nche.edu/media-relations/fact-sheets/nursing-shortage./

Chapter 15
New Traveler Needs Support

Mary is used to coming to work, getting report, organizing her report sheet and meeting her patients' needs. She is very familiar with the logistics of the unit. She's worked on 4 West since graduating from nursing school in 1995. The department head has come to her several times asking her to be the Unit Manager. Mary is not interested in that responsibility.

When Mary arrives to work, she usually goes straight to the locker room, puts her belongings in her locker, checks her patient assignments and waits for the off-going nurse to give report.

Shirley is a travel nurse. She is here on a thirteen-week assignment; this is her first week after orientation. She has been a nurse for two years and feels that travel assignments will allow her to see different parts of the United States and even other countries. She is very excited about nursing and hopes to get an MSN one day.

"It's 10:50 p.m.; I've been sitting here for 10 minutes waiting for the nurse. Sue, do you know who has the patients in Quad A?" Mary asks.

Sue can tell that Mary is already getting a little impatient. She knows Mary very well. "I believe it's Shirley, the new travel nurse. She's been running around the unit all day. Poor thing, she's got the disorganization blues bad."

Mary looks at her watch, then around the room. "Boy is this room a mess," she says out loud to no one in particular. "The coffee pot is dirty, the microwave is dirty, the papers on the bulletin board are outdated. Hopefully I'll get some time tonight and straighten this room up."

"I agree," Sue says. "Shirley and I were saying the same thing."

Shirley bursts through the door. Her hair is messy and her lips are dry. She has a look of fear in her eyes and before she is able to introduce herself and sit down, all the papers in her hands fall to the ground. Mary and Sue exchange glances.

"Oh, hi; I'm Shirley, are you Mary?" Before Mary can answer, Shirley asks, "Are you ready to get report?"

"Yes, I've been waiting for 10 minutes, is it that bad out there?"

"Well maybe it's me," says Shirley. "Okay, Patient in Quad A Room 6 – Barry Friedland, 69; he came in on 5/5 with dx of Ulcerative Colitis. He has D5 NS at 125 cc/hour. He's voiding on his own, he's on Flagyl q 6 and Cipro Q 8. He is using Morphine 1 mg q 2 hours for pain."

"Is he scheduled for a colonoscopy?" Mary asks.

"I don't know," replies Shirley.

"Who is his primary doctor?"

"I don't know," replies Shirley.

"Okay, was he seen by a doctor today?" Mary asks.

"You know, I'm not certain," replies Shirley.

"What about his labs, do you have the labs for the day?"

"Uhm, No. I, oh my gosh, I just remembered something, I'll be right back." Shirley gets up and dashes out the door.

Mary turns to Sue. "Is it me, or am I going to spend the entire first part of my shift cleaning up her mess and figuring out who needs what? Are my patients safe out there with her?"

Sue says nothing.

"Sue, why are you being so quiet? Is Shirley really a nurse?" Sue still says nothing. She looks at Mary and smiles weakly.

"Don't tell me, she's one of those new grads who have a lot of theory and not so much clinical organizational skills," Mary says in disgust.

Shirley rushes back in the room a few minutes later. "Sorry, I needed to switch Mr. Friedland's bag back to the D5 after his antibiotic finished and I also needed to hang a fresh bag because that one was just about finished . . . oh, I have those labs for you too."

The report process was arduous, with Shirley getting up several more times to check on things before finishing report. After all the questions were answered and the "Handing Off" procedure was complete, they left the locker room together.

Mary was at the nursing station checking orders, organizing her report sheet and deciding in what order things needed to be done before the night started.

Shirley turns to her and says, "Mary, I'm really sorry about the not-so-good report I gave you. I'm going to stay until I've completed all the things that need to be done; if you have time, can you show me how you do things on this unit? I hear you are very organized."

There is one class in nursing school that is missing: Organizational Strategies for Nurses.

Systems are crucial if you want to avoid a nursing malpractice lawsuit. If you think of some of the major businesses in the country, you might notice that they take a system that works and use it again and again to grow their bottom line. Most nurses are not in the business to make profits, but we are in the business to stay away from the law.

Nursing malpractice is easy to avoid if you have systems in place. The beginning of your shift is a good place to keep the end in mind. We all want to finish with a good feeling about the way things went. Think positive and put your systems into place.

What are you doing to prepare for the middle of your shift?

Our shifts consist of various activities that are predictable, like medications and treatments. But what about the overwhelming events that pop up unexpectedly — the things that can either take a lot longer than you would have expected or things that require interventions from other people or departments?

If you have patients who are elderly, confused, or on heavy pain medication, you know that safety is key. You know that interacting with these patients is going to carve out pieces of your time in other areas. We are on time constraints throughout the shift. Think about the 98,000 people who are injured in the hospital each year.

Nurses are the largest population of healthcare providers, but unfortunately, there are probably more nurses involved in these lawsuits than any other group. How can we keep our licenses blemish-free? If you researched the licensing board of your state, you would learn about all the nurses who have had their licenses either suspended or revoked. Some deviated from their duties while others might have been innocent; however, the proof lies, to a large extent, in the documentation.

How does a nurse develop systems within the healthcare environment? It begins with the reporting process. Facilities are looking for uniformity in the reporting process. Does your facility have one? If not, develop your own until they do.

In a lawsuit, one of the ways the judicial systems decides if you have deviated from the standard of care is through a timeline chronology. It is no secret in the legal arena that lawyers are looking to reconstruct the events. Did you, the nurse, follow through when a deviation in an assessment was found? Was a healthcare provider notified that there was a change in the patient's condition? Place all of your reporting information on a timeline. Hold yourself accountable for following up or following through on any change in the patient's condition.

As a nurse who spent the majority of her earlier career moving from unit to unit and city to city, I discovered that there is value in asking questions. When you notice a colleague with an effective system, take the parts of that system that can work for you and personalize it. Creating documentation tools and record keeping systems that are specific to your particular area of practice is a key to being organized.

There is no document that speaks to every area in nursing. There is no one system created that captures all the nuances necessary to get it all done right. What is important is knowing what a plaintiff's attorney is looking for in the documentation that would make the case easy to win.

In this case, Shirley needed to reach out to a seasoned nurse with solid organizational skills. She recognized that quality in Mary. Mary had a report sheet designed with her patient population in mind. Not only did it contain all of the signs and symptoms that one looks for as a nurse, but it included a space for labs, tests, calls, therapies and interventions.

The plaintiff's attorney wants to know the "who," "what" and "where" in a case. One of their jobs is to pinpoint where there was a deviation in the standard of care. What, exactly, was the nurse supposed to do that was not done that caused the patient to have a bad outcome? Unless an attorney has gone to medical school or nursing school, they are learning your profession through the entries you've made in the medical record.

Being organized does not mean just doing a thorough assessment and documenting the deviations. It requires follow up with the correct healthcare provider and placing that conversation into your entry. More important than that is the time in which the conversation took place. Organizing your thoughts on the report sheet will assist with your organization when documenting on the medical record and when handing off your patients to the next nurse.

During the reporting or handing off process in this example, Mary asked Shirley questions that Shirley should have known: Who is the patient's doctor? Was the patient seen by a doctor yet today? What are the patient's labs and has anything else been ordered for the patient? Shirley was not able to answer these questions. Could you imagine what it would be like in a deposition situation? Shirley, as the nurse defendant, would be extremely frazzled attempting to prove that she is a competent nurse. We are not expected to have everything in our heads, but having systems to keep track of all that we do is crucial to maintaining accountability in healthcare.

Mary has a reputation of getting things done, to the point that management wanted her to assume the role of charge nurse. Mary is so aware of her strengths and limitations that the prospect of a promotion did not flatter her. She was not interested in a higher salary or more responsibility. She knew what she was comfortable with and it showed. The stress for her was no longer there. That is the place we want to be. But how did she arrive at it? Through her organizational systems.

What could Mary show Shirley? Being a nurse begins with passing the state board exam, but how are we to develop the skills and comfort level of a seasoned nurse? And is it true that nurses eat their young? Well, think back to the beginning of your nursing career when you entered the unit the first time as a "new graduate." Many of the comments your colleagues had beside "congratulations" might have been more along the lines of "let me know if you need anything."

How many nurses are able to make themselves available to the novices? The number is not high. So do we eat our young? We are probably struggling more to place the oxygen mask over our own mouths and noses first.

Mary cannot teach Shirley what will work for Shirley, but Mary *can* simply show Shirley what she does to make her own shifts function so effectively. To strengthen your defensibility, you have to be confident in your approach to care. All of your day-to-day systems need to be considered. Examine what works for you and what doesn't. Drop the bad habits. If there is no one around you who seems to function in a manner you admire, go outside the scope of nursing for ideas on organizing your day, your paperwork and your mind.

Humans thrive on predictability. We are more comfortable when we know what to expect. This theory goes back to birth. Emulate facets of behaviors that you value and leave behind the areas of your practice that bring you stress. Take time to develop documentation systems that will strengthen your professional personality and you will avoid being named in a lawsuit.

Resources:

Glassman, P. (n.d.) Health Literacy [Outreach Section]. *National Network of Libraries of Medicine.* Accessed March 26, 2012 http://nnlm.gov/outreach/consumer/hlthlit.html.

Standard on verbal orders ranks high among common compliance problems. (2009, May). Accessed March 26, 2012 http://www.ncbi.nlm.nih.gov/pubmed/19552346.

Chapter 16
Going Live

When Govi Torres came into the hospital, it wasn't for a colonoscopy. He came in through the ED a few nights ago because he fell off a ladder at his house and landed on his head, then passed out for a few moments. If that wasn't bad enough, during the fall, he scraped up against a nail; this required twenty-six stitches and a tetanus shot. Mr. Torres is worried and frustrated over his fall and his loss of consciousness.

Dr. Grey, Mr. Torres' GI doc, visits him in the hospital. Mr. Torres is told by Dr. Grey that it is time for Mr. Torres' colonoscopy and is asked if it's all right if the colonoscopy is done while he's still in the hospital. Mr. Torres agrees and is prepped for the procedure. Mr. Torres is even willing to allow a bright and ambitious medical student to take part in the procedure. Mr. Torres has had a colonoscopy before and doesn't remember all the details, so he relies on the kindheartedness of Dr. Grey to explain the preparation and procedure again.

Dr. Grey is the youngest member of the GI Practice. He is a very patient man who believes that all patients should be treated with the utmost respect. Dr. Grey is always talking about making certain that patients don't view the healthcare community as adversaries. He spends as much time as possible with his patients and they speak very highly of him.

I saw Dr. Grey go in and out of Mr. Torres' room at least three times today, partly because Mr. Torres is planning on having his colonoscopy done tomorrow and the GI Practice has a set of guidelines they use to prepare their patients. I sat in on the informed consent process, provided Mr. Torres with the literature needed for the test and asked him all the questions on the post-test questionnaire. Mr. Torres got everything right, partly because this facility is conscientious about educating the patients. In fact, if you have a patient needing a lot of education, you are allowed to count that patient as a 1.25 on the census forms instead of a 1.

I was almost certain I was going to be caring for him on the day of his bowel prep, but that's not what happened.

"I hate this, I hate this, I hate this," Lauren says through clenched teeth.

"Hate what?" I ask.

'This computer stuff. I just don't seem to get it."

Lauren has been a nurse here for a long time. She was my preceptor and then became my mentor. She showed me how to organize my assignments, who to watch out for, and how to get to the lab using the back stairway. We don't hang out together outside of work, but anytime there is a work-related event, you can bet we'll be sitting together.

Last year, when the hospital announced we would be going "live," we never thought it was going to happen. But the IT department built a huge building on the campus and they have been working feverishly ever since. The computer orientation program was pretty comprehensive. Lauren and I attended the classes together and that had been a little stressful for me. I didn't understand why people weren't grouped into classes based on their prior computer knowledge. Sitting in the computer lab with people of all different computer skill levels made me antsy, but the worst part was sitting next to Lauren. Lauren is strictly anti-computer. She doesn't own one and has told everyone that she'll never buy one.

"I'd resign," she whispered to me during a "Go Live" training class, "but I need the benefits."

But I didn't understand her problems, because the software is relatively easy. The pages walk you from one item to another.

The hardest part for me might have been the password development stage. The instructor asked us to come up with passwords that have nothing to do with our personal lives, and she said that the passwords shouldn't be a word that's found in the dictionary. It should consist of letters of lower and upper case presentation, numbers and symbols. We were told never to share our passwords because of the HIPAA laws and we were also told to be prepared to change them on a regular basis when prompted by the computer.

Lauren complained about this, too. She said it's hard enough to remember her bank pin number or the pass code on her cell phone.

Getting back to the colonoscopy, I'm not certain what happened, but my assignment was nothing like I expected. Lauren had three of my patients today, including Mr. Torres. "Oh, you have a great assignment," I told her. "I had Torres, Miller and Robinson yesterday. But I thought Robinson was going home; what happened?"

"Oh, he spiked a temp last night," replied Lauren. Then, she changed the subject. "Hey, Mickey, how is it that you understand the computer so well? I am really struggling with it."

"I don't know, but don't worry," I said. "I'll help you. And besides, the IT team is sitting right here at the nurses station. We just went 'live' a few days ago so remember, they're gonna be here for at least another few days. Use them while there here."

As Lauren started to organize her assignment, she looked up at the call board. "Oh, it's Mr. Torres in 2411; time to hit the floor running. I'll catch up with you later, Okay? Maybe we can have lunch together."

"Great," I replied. "Be sure to tell Mr. Torres hello for me. I'll stop by his room if I get a chance."

Just before lunch, I ran into Lauren at the nurses station. She looked exasperated.

"How's it going?" I asked.

"Well, this morning after my assessment, I put all my information into the system."

"Great!" I exclaimed.

"Not so great." Lauren sighed. "Under the GI section, I put in that drop-down box that Mr. Torres is positive for the bowel prep regimen."

"So?" I asked.

"So, he hasn't followed the protocol and I cannot figure out how to amend this stupid machine. He has called me into his room about 49,000 times. I am not so sure between him and his questions and this machine that I can keep being nice. I thought you told me he was a nice man; this is not nice, what he is doing to me."

"Lauren, please calm down," I said firmly. "Is there something I can do to help? Aren't you the one getting your CGRN in a few weeks, though? I know that you know this stuff."

"Yes, I know GI, not computers," Lauren replied, seeming more exasperated than ever. "Oh feathers, there he goes again. I'll be back."

It doesn't seem like there is anything I can say that will help her, but I don't have anything pressing after work, either. I'll make it a point to stay after with her and help her along with the "Go Live" support team.

It had never before occurred to me how frustrating learning new technology can be. I've always taken it for granted. I figured with the way the software is being designed today, the mechanics of the system would be pretty standard. But to a non-computer user, going live must be an incredible challenge. Mickey had just been getting used to the fact that we are going to computerized documentation; up to now, she's taken it for granted. But it is such a learning curve for a non-computer user. After handing off my assignment to the evening nurse, I waited for Lauren at the nurses' station. No one had seen her. She handed off her patients earlier, and then disappeared. Finally I see her down the hall. "Lauren, I've been looking for you," I said.

"Oh, Mickey, I'm not certain what to do. I spoke with the 'Go Live' team and they are willing to sit with me, but the rep for our unit is now helping someone else. Did you say you would walk me through this stuff? I'd really appreciate it." Lauren paused, then went on with, "In fact, for being such a good friend, I'd like to give you my ticket to the 'Scrap Book Convention' next week at the downtown convention center."

"Lauren, you don't have to do that," I told her. "I just want to help you."

"No, Mickey. I'll only let you help me if you take the ticket."

"Okay, I'll take the ticket," I said. "Thank you so much."

We met back at the terminals and logged on, side-by-side. I started looking for the program Lauren hadbeen working on. I figured it wouldn't be long until I got used to it.

The support person was still working with a nurse from the evening shift and they looked like they were going to be a while, but I figured this couldn't be that difficult.

Lauren had logged on to her patient census and she's completing some of the other information needed for her charting. She has always been very conscientious about her documentation. She told me a couple of stories about nurses and malpractice. To me, it sounds like if the nurse can defend him or herself through the documentation, then there is a pretty good chance that the nurse has nothing to worry about. If the documentation tells a non-fiction story with ample follow up and interventions, then the nurse should not have to worry.

Lauren has been a wealth of information for me. Now, I wanted to help her.

I glanced over at the IT rep and noticed that the other nurse is finishing up. I want to run over to the IT person before another nurse has a question.

I turned to Lauren and asked her to keep an eye on this terminal for me. I told her that I'm walking over to get help. As I got up and walked away, I got this funny feeling that I should have logged off. The IT team had made that very clear. They've told us time and time again that logging off when you get up is as important as wearing a seat belt when driving. Many of the computer techs have said that you are in the driver's seat while logged on and you wouldn't want to give anyone else the keys to your car, so don't let anyone else enter information while using your pass code.

Just as I get to Ms. IT, another nurse slipped in front. "Oh, I just have a quick question," she said, and asked it before anyone else could speak.

Great, I think to myself, *I get to learn another fact about the software that I didn't know!*

Finally, it's my turn. "Mary, I have a question about the

GI prep program. Could you please help us? Lauren and I are logged in at the East Hall Computer Room."

As we walked toward the East Hall, my computer assistant is stopped yet again by another of my colleagues. She let me know that she would be right behind me.

As I walked down the hall, I looked into the room where I was logged on. I noticed that Lauren was sitting at the terminal I had been using. The first thing I thought is that maybe she remembered to log me off, so she's using her own password to work under.

As I entered the room, I noticed that her body language changed and she stiffened up. I had this very uncomfortable feeling. When I leaned over her shoulder, I noticed that she was making changes under my name.

"Lauren, are you logged on under my password?" I asked.

"Um, yea, I didn't think you'd mind," Lauren said. "I noticed that you had accessed the GI prep program and once I scrolled down to room 2411, I was able to input the timeline of events for Mr. Torres. I made a note stating that I had reported off to you."

I couldn't believe what Lauren had just said.

But she'd continued on. "Isn't this great? Thanks so much for helping me. You are gonna have a great time at the Scrap Book Convention next week."

"Lauren, we gotta talk," I said.

As much as I had wanted to go to the Convention, I was so mad at Lauren that I had to make certain I chose my words carefully.

This is a difficult situation to be in. You have computer skills and your colleague doesn't. There are so many variables that contribute to a person's ability to grasp the concept of using a computer. Mickey had to make a decision that could affect her friendship, but acting legally and ethically is always the best decision.

The electronic medical record is not designed to confuse, frustrate or turn good people into bad, but, for an inanimate object, it can create emotional distress. EMRs are designed to create "meaningful use." That means that, although the systems seem disjointed and at times nonsensical, there is a clear method to its madness.

Knowing the grand scheme of things is very helpful. According to Dr. Amy Barton, a nursing professor at the University of Colorado Denver (2011), there are five patient safety goals. They are:

1. Improve quality, safety, and efficiency and reduce health disparities.
2. Engage patients and families.
3. Improve care coordination.
4. Improve population and public health.
5. Ensure adequate privacy and security provisions for personal health information.

Like most major changes and overhauls, there are systematic steps required to reach the ultimate goals. This is another reason for the development of your personal and professional nurse tracking tools to mature during these times of electronic medical record implementation.

Dr. Patricia McCartney (2010), a nurse who specializes in information technology, outlines the process of technological integration in healthcare. She states there are eight steps to the adaptation of the EMR. There are three major players in the system: pharmacy, laboratory and radiology. When all are completely integrated, the system is considered adapted.

Along the continuum, the departments bring the nursing component and other ancillary departments in. It is like a loop system, and each time the loop makes a circle, it picks up another piece of a department. Nursing integration is not always done during one cyclical pattern. Depending on your facility, you might lose all paper at once, or over time, or transition from paper-light to paperless.

In the above example with Lauren and Mickey, it seems like Mickey has a strong grasp on the EMR. But the only way to really know how anyone is doing is via a chart audit. I recall being audited and did not like the feeling of someone criticizing my work. But at the time, I didn't realize it was an opportunity to learn about documentation expectations.

According to Nurse Frankie Wong (2009), the best time to audit charts and teach nurses about their documentation discrepancies is as soon after the entries as possible. For example, 24 hours after the entries are better than 24 days. This enables the nurse to have better recollection of the events.

The audit process is one to embrace. Instead of shying from the auditors and running when you see them coming, make it known that you want to be audited. Use the auditors to learn more about your documentation style in order to further develop your strategy sheet so that it matches the facility expectations.

This becomes even more apparent when looking at documentation from a litigious viewpoint. Cases are examined years after the event and recollection fades over time. Better recollection of the events creates more accurate documentation. And if your chart has been audited by your facility, it emphasizes that your entries are closest to the expected standard of documentation.

EMRs are systems that have specific indications, paths, language and patterns. Understanding the strategic plan for its implementation and audit process will support your goals to become a more efficient nurse documenter.

In this chapter's example, Lauren probably needs to spend more time with the IT professionals and less time complaining. The nursing informatics department has the information needed to assist you with the integration of your strategic plan and theirs.

Resources:

McCartney, P. R. (2010, Nov/Dec). Benchmarking electronic medical record adoption. [Health Information Technology column]. *MCN, American Journal of Maternal Child Nursing 35*(6), 358. DOI: 10.1097/NMC.0b013e3181f0f3d6.

Wong, F. (2009) Chart audit. *Journal for Nursing in Staff Development,* 25(2), E1-E6. DOI: 10.1097/NND.0b013e31819e11fa.

Chapter 17
Family Discord in the Pediatric Unit

Brigitte Scott, RN, has been a pediatric nurse for about six years. She has received report from the ED nurse.

"They just got off the elevator," Brigitte says as she sees her patient being wheeled on a stretcher down the hall. The patient's dad is in tow, his hands full of dolls, a grey furry elephant and a pink knapsack. He looks tired, worried and disheveled. Not unusual, thinks Brigitte.

The nurse from the ED called about 20 minutes ago with report. "Hi Brigitte, it's Khadijah down in the ED. I have a patient for you; are you ready to take report?"

"Yup, let me have it," Brigitte says.

"Jasmine Johnson is 25 months old. She's being admitted for fever of unknown origin. Her dad said she didn't sleep at all last night and was moaning and restless. She's had a few sips of juice since yesterday but nothing to eat."

Khadijah pauses until Brigitte tells her to keep going.

Khadijah continues with, "He gave her two doses of acetaminophen during the night. He says her temp never went below 101F so he brought her in. She hasn't voided since she's been here, which would be about two hours. Her dad states that the last time he remembers changing her diaper was last night around 9pm."

"Vitals?" Brigitte asks.

"V/S 101.2, 110, 90/50, 24. I gave her acetaminophen an hour ago; it's on the MAR. She has an IV to her Left AC, with D5 NS at 50 cc/hour. The line was very difficult to start, so please be careful."

"Got it," Brigitte says.

Khadijah continues, "She's being admitted under Dr. London's service. The father isn't certain, but thinks she might have had a seizure. There is a strong history of seizures on his side. The docs want to tap her as soon as the consent is signed. I think that's it. Any questions?"

"Yes," Brigitte says. "Where's her mom?"

"Oh, well the story is, they are separated and this is dad's weekend. She's on her way in."

Jasmine and her dad are settled into the room. Brigitte does an assessment on the patient and starts the paperwork. During the process, Brigitte mentions that Dr. London would like to do a spinal tap once the consent has been signed.

"No problem" says Mr. Johnson. "I will do whatever it takes to make sure she is all right."

At the completion of the admission process, Brigitte tells Mr. Johnson that she'll call Dr. London's service and have a resident come up to explain the procedure. She assures him that she will be in the room to witness the process and make certain that all his questions are answered before he signs.

The resident arrives. "I'm Rona Scott, the resident covering Dr. London's service this weekend. I'm looking for Jasmine Johnson's nurse; I'm here to obtain consent for the spinal tap."

"Great, I'm Brigitte Scott, her nurse. The dad is in the room waiting for us."

As the healthcare team enters the room, the father places a finger to his lips, "Shhhh," he whispers, "she's finally asleep. Can we talk right outside the door?"

"Sure," replies Dr. Scott. They walk outside the room.

"Now," Dr. Scott continues in a quiet voice, "we understand that your daughter might have had a seizure. Febrile seizures or seizures associated with fever are not uncommon in children your daughter's age. Many times a seizure is an isolated incident that might never happen again."

The father nods.

Dr. Scott continues. "Sometimes, seizures are caused by an infection in the spinal fluid, and then sometimes children have a seizure and it will be the beginning of more seizures because of misfiring in the brain. Is it true that there is a history of seizures in your family?"

"Yes," says Jasmine's father.

"Well, let me explain the process of a spinal tap, and please ask as many questions as you have," Dr. Scott says. "Brigitte, your nurse, will be available to clarify any other questions you might think of after I leave. If she cannot answer them, she can call me. Now what about your daughter's mother; is she here?"

"No," Jasmine's father states. "She'll be here shortly and I know she wants what's best for our daughter also. How soon can this be done? I'm anxious to know if she has a spinal infection."

The spinal tap process is explained and the consent is signed by Jasmine's father. Brigitte Scott, RN, signs as the witness.

Several moments later, Vanessa Johnson, Jasmine's mother, walks off the elevator. She is searching for the nurses station and finds someone to direct her to Jasmine's room. Once in there, it is obvious that she does not agree with the informed consent for the spinal tap. Mrs. Johnson calls Brigitte into the room.

"Are you a mother?" Vanessa Johnson asks Brigitte.

"Yes," replies Brigitte. "I am. Why?"

"Besides being an inconsiderate and incompetent nurse, you have violated my right as a parent; I did not and will not approve of my daughter having a spinal tap. You know I can sue you for Failure to Consent. I'd like to see the doctor and your supervisor."

Did Brigitte do something wrong? What should her documentation include?

We walk a fine line when working with families. We must be able to be a part of the process without being burdensome and confrontational, yet when we reach out a hand with information and psychosocial support, is that all that's required?

No, it's not.

If you consider the makeup of the family dynamics, the pre-existing conflicts and the medical dilemma at hand, according to the Nursing Code of Ethics, Brigitte was in violation. All parts of the family should have been in attendance for the consent process. The scenario does not indicate that the nurse was advocating for the entire patient/family unit to be present.

Nurse Margaret Kelly states in her study that was published in 2007 that pediatric and neonatal nurses are required to formulate the care plan using the desires of the caregivers. She states that using a negotiated care model (NCM), the healthcare provider is able to take all parties into consideration. More importantly, it is the documentation derived from these conversations that will allow for all assumptions to be removed. The study goes on to explain that relationships and expectations cannot be taken for granted. This, along with contemporaneous documentation throughout the healthcare encounter, will alleviate misconceptions and potential lawsuits.

Perhaps, in our example, the established relationships and expectations could have been handled differently. It is difficult for a facility to have all systems in place to anticipate disgruntled recipients of care, but if you work in an environment with minors, please be aware that management of their care relies on your ability to partner with all parties to create an outcome that satisfies the standard of nursing practice.

If you work in an environment where the patients do not have the authority to make decisions for themselves, are there systems in place that delineate how issues are to be addressed? What information can you track on your strategy sheet that would support your intentions of making a comprehensive care plan?

Resources:

Kelly, M. (2007). Achieving family-centered care: Working on or working with stakeholders. *Neonatal, Pediatric and Child Health Nursing, 3*(4). 11.

Chapter 18
My Patient, Mrs. Difficult

Freda Nichols is a 60-year-old woman who comes into the facility at least once per season. I've been here about five years and I've probably taken care of her about three or four times. I know she's been here other times because I've heard other nurses talk about her in report and at the nurses station. She doesn't usually have any visitors and doesn't want social service intervening. She thinks they are just being nosey and really don't care about her and all her problems.

I was not her nurse today, but I heard Melissa yelling over my shoulder. "I'll be right there, Mrs. Nichols." Then she turned to me and said, "Listen, I have Mrs. Nichols today. Wanna trade some of your patients with me?"

I started to laugh, but Melissa didn't think it was funny. She looked at me as if she wanted to cry. We have all had awful experiences with Mrs. N She appears really nice, but there is something about her that spooks us all. We all feel like she is one of those patients who want to make her fortune as a plaintiff in a high-profile nursing malpractice lawsuit. We are all potential defendants and are well aware of it, but when it comes to Mrs. N, we feel the pressure to perform like our license depends on it. And it does.

"Sorry, Mel, not today. I've already started and didn't eat a hearty enough breakfast to deal with her. Listen, if you need any help, I'm here for you; you know that, right?"

"Yeah, right."

It was busy on 6 East today. It turned out that the state made a surprise visit to the hospital, and they were walking around here a little upset. There was a report that the food service department had several complaints and the state came to investigate. They usually spend three or four days here during these calls, and we were almost certain this visit meant they would interview the patients at their bedside about their food.

Whenever there is a call from the state about a certain department, whether it is food service, maintenance, nursing or human resources, the entire facility is up in arms. We never know if they are going to find something that could trigger them to expand their investigation to include a department that wasn't the original concern.

The food has been poor lately, but there are always patients complaining about their food in the hospital. Let's face it, hospital food has never really had a great reputation.

But patients and families have been saying things that I've never heard before. The other day, a patient's wife told me that the mashed potatoes were not only cold, they were frozen. She couldn't put her fork through it to feed her husband. She was really upset because she didn't have any money to buy him something from the cafeteria. I called down to the kitchen, but, by the time they brought up another plate, he had lost his appetite. Another patient told me that her sandwich looked like someone had taken a bite out of it. I tried to explain that was the natural shape of the bread. She told me that if that is true, I should probably go into another line of work, like making toys for Santa. We both laughed and I then I called down to the kitchen to have another sandwich sent up.

The morning flew by and as I was getting ready to take a break, I noticed Mel at the nurses station. Her hair was disheveled and her lips were dry. "Mel, how's it going?"

"I am not having a very good day," she said. "And the more the day goes on, the more uncomfortable and unsure of myself I get. I think Mrs. N is taking medication from home and I am not sure, but I think she might be using alcohol."

"Well, she is a documented alcoholic; that is probably in all of the admission paperwork every time she comes in."

"No. I mean, yes, I know that." Mel pauses and tries to gather her thoughts. "What I'm saying is that I believe she is drinking right now; her breath smells of alcohol. I also think she has a stash of her own narcs. She complains about back pain all the time. I never seem to be able to get her to a comfortable and acceptable pain score. She takes and tolerates more pain medication then anyone I've ever cared for. The only time I think she is comfortable is when she's asleep and it is those times that I get nervous and have to check her breathing to make certain she is alive."

I must have chuckled, because the next thing I knew, Mel was telling me to stop laughing.

"Karleen, it's not funny," Mel insisted.

"I'm not laughing at you," I explained. "I want you to laugh with me." I paused, then said, "Mel, you are a great nurse and you know what you're doing. Just make certain that your documentation is on point and you shouldn't have any trouble with our 'Ms. Potential Plaintiff'."

"When is the last time you took care of her?" Mel asked.

"I'm not certain," I said, "It must have been a few months ago. Why?"

"Well, you know she is a type 2 diabetic."

I nodded.

"Well, her AIC is now 8.5 and the docs want to put her on insulin, but she is not interested in learning how to do it. She wants no part of the injection routine." Mel frowned. "Not only that, she has a tiny dark area on her right great toe, and I am afraid she might never leave this place."

I laughed again, quietly.

"Karleen, please stop laughing at me."

"Well, stop being so funny," I told her. "I said before that I am here for you; all I can say now is to make certain that your documentation speaks for itself. Remember, you are a non-fiction writer and you must create a document that reads in as a high definition, Blu-ray movie."

"Yes," Mel said, "but with this electronic charting, it's difficult to see the finished picture."

"I know, but guess what? I created this paper template of our software." I showed Mel the paper.

"It's really quite nice," she said.

"What I did was to write down all the categories the computer asks me for so that I can make certain that all of the patient's issues have been addressed. That way, I don't answer the same questions in two different places two different ways. I'll make you a copy. Do you think that will help?"

"It can't hurt," Mel says firmly. "I don't know if you know this, Karleen, but Mrs. N came in this time because she blacked out while driving. Well, she wasn't driving; she said she felt herself losing consciousness and pulled over. As it turned out, she said there was an ambulance in the parking lot and they were able to get her here."

I nodded again. "Did the tests find anything at all?"

"No." Mel frowned again. "The labs and tests couldn't determine why she blacked out, but I think it might have to do with all of the doctor shopping she does. She has four or five primary doctors listed on her chart." Mel looked at her watch. "Listen, I've gotta go; please pick me up a sandwich when you go down and bring me a copy of your computer cheat sheet and I'll take a quick break when you get back. Thanks." She rushed off.

A few hours later, I returned from a break.

"Karleen, I am glad you're back," Mel said. "The state asked for charts on this unit. You know they are looking for people who can talk intelligently to them, right? Well, they are going to interview Mrs. N Can this day get any worse?"

"Mel, stop!" I told her. "You're gonna make me laugh again. Now, here is your sandwich; give me report on your patients and, oh, here is the information that you should use when charting." I handed her my paper cheat sheet.

While Mel was on break, I began to feel her pain. Her assignment was pretty hectic, as it had been before the state made several trips on the 6 East. They asked for, and took, Mrs. N's chart. Then they asked for the nurse caring for her. I spoke to them, letting them know that I was covering for Melissa and could answer all their questions. They were pretty nice about this initial interview, but decided to wait for her to return before they asked the remaining questions.

Also, as luck would have it, the lab called with some critical values for the infamous Mrs. N I called the doctor covering and wrote a note in the chart. In my note, I made reference to covering for Melissa while she was on break. In nursing documentation, it is always prudent to speak to the chart like speaking to an elementary school child. People who read these charts have not always been to nursing school and the easier it is for them to follow along, the better off the person making the entry will be.

"Okay, Melissa, where are you? It's been 45 minutes and the state is due back anytime," I thought to myself. By this time, I have really felt her pain, but took her report sheet and continued to write the progression or digressions of her patients on the sheet.

When Melissa finally came back, she was rested and revived. She had a huge smile on her face. She was carrying a large cup of coffee in one hand and the report sheet I gave her in the other. "Thank you so much for the time and the information," she said. "I really needed both."

"You're welcome," I told her.

Melissa kept talking. "This document makes so much sense. Having the categories in your hand and not having to guess what is coming next makes documentation seem so much easier. I usually struggle with trying to remember if the software has asked me these questions already or if what I am answering is for another patient. Thank you, thank you, thank you."

"Don't thank me too much," I said. "Wait until I tell you what's happened since you've been gone."

I gave her all the information: the state wanting to talk to her before talking to Mrs. N, the critical labs, and the call I'd made to the doctor and the doctor's orders.

Melissa didn't look as happy as she had before, but was grateful just the same. "Let me check on Mrs. N before the state comes back. I really don't want to tell her that the state wants to interview her, but I'll try my best to help her see how wonderful and important she is to the whole process of healthcare." She walked away, and related the following conversation to me later.

"Hi, Mrs. N How are you feeling now?" Melissa asked.

"I feel lousy, I always feel lousy and it's you people around here that never seem to know what's wrong with me. I'm sure my insurance company pays you good money to take care of me and I never seem to get any better. I just end right back up in this place no matter what I do. Do you think I like being here? Don't answer that because you don't know me and you don't know my situation."

Mrs. N went on with, "I worked forty years for the government. I never took a vacation nor called out sick. I was a good worker and now look at me. I practically live in the hospital and the food here stinks."

"You think the food here stinks, Mrs. N.?" Melissa asked.

"Yes, it stinks," Mrs. N said emphatically. "You work here; you see what the food looks like. I am always hungry. Maybe that is one of the reasons I always end up back in here, but I can't heal because of the lousy food."

"Mrs. N, would you like to speak to someone about the food that might be able to help make some changes for you?"

"Yeah, sure, whatever," Mrs. N answered. "You people are always promising things and all I ever see is the same people doing the same things all the time. Last time I was here, I asked to see someone about the food and they sent me a girl no bigger than my cane to come and talk to me. She looked like she was still in high school. What does she know about food?"

"Mrs. N, there is someone very important who wants to talk to you about the food," Mel replied. "But they are just interested in the food, nothing else, and we thought you would be a great person to talk to. Now, I'm going to check you over one more time and make certain you feel well before bringing them in. Can I get you anything? How is your pain?"

"My pain? Oh, its all right—right now. Don't worry, I'll let you know when I need something, thank you. Hey, how do I look? Should I put on lipstick for these 'important' people?"

"No, Mrs. N You look as beautiful, as you always do."

Melissa was laughing when she walked out of Mrs. N's room.

"Mel, what happened in there?" I asked. "You're smiling; no, you're . . . laughing?"

"Well I found some common ground with the patient and told her that some important people want to talk to her about what she thinks is wrong with the food," Mel replied. "We kinda had a nice time together. I'm gonna write my notes while all this is still fresh in my head. Will you be around if I need you?"

"Of course," I said.

Writing notes while the information is fresh in your mind is one of the best things a documenter can do. Police officers, reporters and journalists are some professions that need to take notes about events as they are occurring. Some people take notes afterward, while others have the luxury of recording events directly as they occur.

Nurses cannot take notes "on the spot" very often. Instead, too often, we must rely on our memories when it comes down to documentation. The law asks the nurse to make entries as contemporaneously as possible. Using quotations in documentation adds credibility to the story and the timeline of events.

But what should Melissa do about a patient who is non-compliant with behavior and is possibly self-medicating with pills and alcohol while a patient in the hospital?

We always have a duty to the safety of the patient. Is it *safe* for Mrs. N to be self-medicating? Of course not. The methods to manage that, and the repercussions that follow, should be closely tied to your documentation.

Chapter 19
Standard of Practice for All

Renatta was just about to leave for her shift at work when the house phone rang. *"Who could that be?"* she thought. The kids were all home and their friends usually texted each other. It could be a solicitor. Just to be on the safe side, she decided to check the caller ID before leaving the house. The number was from Parker House, the skilled facility she worked for.

"Hello," said her co-worker, Joaquim.

"Oh, Joaquim, why are you calling me on this phone?" Renatta couldn't help but ask.

"I have been trying to get you on your cell, but it just kept going into voice mail. Listen; I've been here since 7 a.m.; I'm doing a double today and I'll see you when you get here, but I just had to let you know what was going on before you came in." Joaquim took a breath, and went on. "Do you remember last month when we noticed something unusual with Adam Simms?"

"Who is Adam Simms? Oh, you mean the PA? Yeah, I remember him. What about him?"

"Well, all I can tell you is that what you thought about him was right," Joaquim said. "This morning, Dr. Spears came through and she was asking about all the orders that Adam had written. She wanted a list of the patients who were on her service last month because of some questions about the orders that Adam wrote. I'll tell you the rest when you get in. Let's get together sometime tonight, Okay?"

Renatta got off the phone, mumbling something or other. She felt shocked; with her mouth hanging open, she walked into her bathroom and closed the door. She still had her bag hanging on her shoulder—the bag she won during that raffle at the hospital. There had been a nursing appreciation luncheon that day. No, it hadn't been in May during Nurses Week, it had been just before Christmas.

Renatta and Joaquim had decided to take their lunch together that day. As they were walking to the appreciation luncheon, they overheard Adam Simms and another PA.

They were saying something about not waiting for labs to come back before writing orders, and their conversation was pretty intense. The other PA told Simms that he was asking for trouble if he did that. "Not only will the reimbursement be in question," the other PA said, "but that is a potential lawsuit waiting to happen."

Renatta knew that lawsuits happen all the time for things like stating that the labs were within normal limits when tests haven't yet come back from the lab. When the two PAs had realized that Renatta and Joaquim had stopped to listen to their conversation, they turned to each other and started laughing. Then they asked Renatta and Joaquim to mind their own business before they had walked away.

Renatta stared at herself in the mirror. She'd never forget that day; this pocketbook reminds her about it all the time.

"Oh, I've gotta go," she said out loud to herself, before yelling to her kids, "See you later. Daddy will be home in about fifteen minutes. I love you."

"We love you, too, Mom," her oldest son, Tim, yelled back. "We haven't forgotten what you said earlier, either; something about always doing your best, even if it means making difficult decisions?"

Renatta mumbled something back, then escaped to her car. She got in, turned on the ignition, and put on her seat belt. Before backing out of the driveway, she decided to look at her cell phone. Joaquim said that he had tried to call her and it went right to her voice mail. *"I wonder if anyone else was trying to call me,"* she thought.

She fished for her phone, as it had fallen to the bottom of her purse, and turned it on. The LCD light warmed up and finally her phone was connected to the cell tower. She had three new messages. *"Three?"* she thought to herself. *"Who else might be trying to reach me? I've been home with the kids all day."* She decided to check the messages before placing her car in reverse. *"Oh, it's getting late,"* she thought, *but I really have to find out who called me."*

Renatta is one of those nurses who have a lot of acquaintances. Her colleagues really like her, because she usually remains impartial to most anything that is gossip at work. She had always been clear on her boundaries. She knew that if you do your best to follow the rules about nursing and healthcare, you could expect to stay out of trouble. Her husband calls her, "Judge Renatta." He liked to hold court and have her make the final decisions about family issues. Of their four children, two were already teenagers and their relationship with them was very special. Her kids actually wanted to stay home most weekends and hang out with each other. It was like that at work, too. People respected her opinions and her advice.

The first message was from her mother. She wanted Renatta to call her about the plumbing problem she was having. The second phone call was from Joaquim; he said he would try her at home and then hung up. The third call was from Adam Simms.

Before Renatta listened to the message, she wondered how in Heck he had her cell phone number. Adam asked that she see him whenever she got into work, and asked that she not mention his request to anyone. He left his cell phone number and the times that he would be around this evening.

Renatta felt devastated about all this, because she knows Adam. She understands that Joaquim saw Adam that day, and in the past she'd heard him and another PA talking about fudging lab values to get their work finished earlier. But there is no way Adam could know about all the other things she had noticed about his ethics and practice.

The first time Renatta had began to suspect that this PA was not practicing according to the codes and standards as listed in the CMS guidelines and the PA standards of practice was about six months ago. She'd been working on 3B when Adam had come around to make his rounds. She remembered that it had been a Sunday morning and very quiet. All the aides had gathered their linen and supplies and had begun their assignments. There were no other nurses around.

Renatta had been in the med room, which is located behind the nurses station. It had been like being in a bathroom stall when someone else walks in. If you are quiet, someone else might not realize that he isn't alone.

In this case, Adam had gathered his charts before sitting down to document. Renatta hadn't seen him on the unit before he sat down, and didn't think that he had made any assessments regarding his patients, but she hadn't really been paying attention. Renatta remembered that she had stayed quiet while she prepared her meds and documented some notes.

Then she had heard Adam's cell phone vibrate; Adam's chair moved when he stood up. She peeked out the door and noticed that he had looked down both hallways of the unit, as if to determine if the coast were clear. When he sat back down, he enjoyed a conversation with someone he was obviously trying to impress — someone not in healthcare, probably someone he was interested in dating.

Renatta had tried to stop listening because she had her own work to do, but then Adam had mentioned his title. He told the person on the phone that as a "doctor" the staff had to follow his orders, and that the patients and families are always honored when he stopped in to see them.

"A 'doctor'?" Renatta thought. *"Had she really heard Adam say that?"*

Renatta stopped what she was doing and peeked out the door again. She noticed Adam's posture as he spoke; his chest was out and his head was held high. She wondered how many other people he had lied to about his profession, and what orders he had written that were not approved by his attending.

Renatta had tried to forget about this, but it was exactly these types of things that began to add up and affect the patients and staff. What he had said to that person on the phone wasn't just a joke between him and the person on the phone, and it certainly hadn't been just a jovial conversation he was having with another PA. Adam's behavior, or way of thinking, had begun to spill over into real life.

Renatta knew right there and then that something needed to be done about Adam, but what? She had seen no evidence thus far that indicated that a patient had been injured or affected by Adam's orders.

This was when Renatta decided to keep a little notebook with anecdotal notes about Adam. She knew that if their paths ever crossed, and if there was a question about her nursing judgment, this notebook could help her prove her case.

Healthcare policy is a beast. It would be great if nursing came with a set of instructions that gave directions about what we are supposed to do and what specific roles everyone else needs to play in the great scheme of things. Unfortunately, it doesn't work that way. Rules and regulations are changing according to the healthcare climate. If there were no rules, and people always used their best judgement to make decisions while caring for people, we would have a fundamental notion of what the expectations are.

Policies and procedures are the rule makers in healthcare. So, in this chapter's example, what is the role of the physician's assistant supposed to be? It sounds simple, but here it is: the same as everyone else's. PAs should follow the standard of care and document truthful entries only.

Renatta thought back to the last time she had to look up a policy on the Parker House Web site. She recalled how there had been so many pages with all sorts of different buttons to negotiate. She kept telling herself that she would spend more time learning the policies and procedures that specifically applied to her job. But knowing all of that didn't negate the fact that Adam Simms had been writing orders before getting labs, and that he had been telling people that he was a doctor rather than a PA.

When Renatta pulls into Parker House parking lot, she is seven minutes late. "Oh, I hate being late," she says out loud. She finds a parking space, jumps out and locks the door. *"Doggone it,*

I forget my lunch in the car," she thought as she walked into the building. *"I'll get it later."*

She punched in and ran to 3B. As she settled into pre-conference, she heard her name being paged over the loudspeaker. "Renatta Pierce, call 6673; Renatta Pierce, please dial 6673." Renatta thought, *"Whoever that is can wait."*

Renatta said aloud, "Marie, please continue with report; that page can wait."

Marie was the off-going nurse and was upset because it was late and she should have gone home ten minutes ago. Her husband was waiting downstairs for her, and their ten-month-old child was in the car with a slight temperature. Marie could hardly wait to get out of there.

As they continued the report process, Renatta heard her name over the loudspeaker again. "Renatta Pierce, please dial 6673. Renatta Pierce, please dial 6673."

Renatta thought, *"Oh my goodness, who could be paging me? I just got here!"* But aloud, she said, "Excuse me, Marie. I know you have to leave, but this must be important. Let me just get whoever it is off the phone and come back so you can leave." Renatta got to the nearest phone and called 6673. "Hello, this is Renatta Pierce; is someone there paging me?"

"Hold on, let me check." The woman who answered the phone muffles it before calling out, "Is someone paging Renatta Pierce?"

There is a one-minute wait that feels like five minutes. Finally, there is a strange voice that came onto the phone. "This is Adam Simms."

"Adam, are you paging me? This is Renatta Peirce."

"Yes, Renatta, I need to talk to you. What time can I come down there?"

"Look Adam, I just got here and I am in report. I don't have any time to speak with you tonight." She hung up before he had the chance to say another word. She didn't know exactly what

Adam wanted to talk about, but she knew it must have to do with him falsifying records, considering he seemed desperate to speak with her.

Renatta went back to the conference room in order to finish getting report. She felt defeated, but knew that it takes courage to do the right thing. Considering all the things she had ever done in nursing, she felt comfortable and had no regrets.

Chapter 20
Decisions and Demands from Out of State

"Hello, thank you for calling Shady Rest Assisted Living. This is Lydia; how may I direct your call?"

"Hi, Lydia, this is Tammy Taulten. My mother, Emma Jean Taulten, is a resident there, but she was taken to the hospital last night; the nursing director wasn't available yesterday and the message left on my voice mail wasn't clear. I'm not quite sure why my Mom was sent to the hospital. No one seems to have an explanation. So, is the director in now?"

"Yes, I'll transfer you," Lydia said.

The director informed Tammy about what the director had been told. "Your mother was found in the main kitchen. She had the gas stove on, and said she needed to start cooking for the party. She was extremely agitated. I know that is out of character for your mother. We kept redirecting her, but she kept wandering in the hallways. The night staff called the on-call nurse, who thought your mom might have a UTI and decided to have her evaluated at the hospital. We tried to contact you, but just got your voice mail. How is she doing?"

"Oh, she's all right," Tammy said. "They did cultures and are waiting for results; so far, they told me that Mom was dehydrated." Then Tammy hung up the phone in disbelief. What now, mother? she thinks.

The phone rang at the nurses station. The caller, a woman, asked to speak with the nurse caring for Mrs. Emma Jean Taulten, and stated that she was her sister from out of state. She gave the code word, which allowed her to receive information about her mother without violating HIPPA law. She also made it clear that she is an RN and would like to be involved with all aspects of her mother's care.

The nurse gives her a report. "Your mother came in last evening confused and agitated; she was very resistant to care and repeated the phase 'dinner will be late'. She is resting quietly now."

"What meds is she on?" Asks Melissa Sutton, the daughter from out of state.

"She has an IV going at 75 cc/hour, she's on Ativan for agitation and Cipro for the infection."

"Have the cultures come back positive for an infection?"

"No, but the doctors wanted to start her on something just in case —"

Melissa interrupted the nurse. "Who is her doctor?"

The nurse felt defensive, but gave all the information requested by the sister before hanging up. Then, she turns to her colleague, "That was the out of town daughter! Need I say more?"

The doctors met with Tammy and explained their findings. The neurologist had determined that her mother was a perfect candidate for a study they are doing with Clioquinoline. It is being used in the treatment of dementia. Tammy agrees to enroll her mother in the study. The nurse is available to assist with the consent and answer all the questions. Tammy understands that this medication might not help her mother, but feels that it cannot hurt.

Several days later the nurses are handing off report at the change of shift.

"Room 417, Mrs. Emma Jean Taulten 83 y/o newly dx with dementia, started on Clioquinoline, no adverse side effects noted, no agitation or unusual outbursts. IV still running and she was positive for a UTI, antibiotics are piggybacked q 6 and on schedule." She paused, then went on with, "The daughter from out of state called five times today. Each time she called, I was more and more upset. It was so busy today and she called and literally cursed me out for the care that we have been giving her mother. She repeatedly told me that she was to be notified before her mother was placed on any new medication and especially an experimental medication. She reiterated several times that she did not sign up for the study. She made me feel like I had done something very wrong. She told me that her fiancé is a lawyer and she's not afraid to use his position to get results.."

The oncoming nurse asks "What did you document?"
"Everything!"

Documentation has to allow the reader (another healthcare professional, an attorney, or a jury of your peers) to bring the words into a three-dimensional scenario. The reader has to be able to hear your side of the story before you have to appear on the witness stand.

Here is an example of the documentation:

8:30 a.m. – TCF SOOO - Call w/all changes to pt. R - as time permits. SOI will have all info.

10:30 a.m. TCF OOSO, multiple Q re: MD visits.

11 a.m. Dr. Wang in, msg re SOOO given.

2:30 p.m. TCF SOOO, Re: MD again. Msg given to Dr. Wang.
In a loud tone, "Your damn hospital! All you do is turn people into experiments."

4:30 p.m. TCF SOOO, raised voice. "If the doctor taking care of my mother does not call by the end of the day, and something happens to my mother, I will sue you and this facility, please have the doctor call me," then she hung up.

5:30 p.m. SOI in. TCF SOOO explained. "Sorry, that is her typical behavior, next time she calls, tell her to call me."

6 p.m. TCF SOOO - "Did I mention that my fiancé is a medical malpractice plaintiff attorney?" I thanked her and hung up.

Key: – TCF - Telephone call from
SOOO - Out of state significant other
R - Reply
SOI - Significant other instate
Q - questions

Chapter 21
Unwitnessed Fall at the Skilled Facility

Mrs. Claire Bradshaw had been an upstanding citizen of the area since anyone could remember. She taught at the elementary school and there were some employees at the facility who remember her because she was their teacher. She had a terrific imagination and had a special way of interacting with the children; it's a shame that she was diagnosed with dementia a few years ago and is now confined to our skilled nursing facility.

Today, Mrs. Bradshaw is still quite independent. She walks the hallway several times per day, telling everyone she passes that she's on her way to the teachers' lounge. When she needs some fresh air, she'll tell the staff it's time for recess. And, up until recently, she had not been considered either an elopement or fall risk.

Mrs. Bradshaw's four children are involved with her care. They take turns attending care planning meetings, and they are always around during holidays and birthdays. They all live about twenty minutes away and you can expect them to visit after any of them gets a call about a change in Mrs. Bradshaw's condition. They've been easy to get along with, except for one time when Mrs. Bradshaw developed a really bad rash that covered 90% of her body. It took months to heal and she had to be hospitalized twice because of it. The family was so upset, they threatened to call the state and have her transferred to another facility. After that, things were not quite the same between the Bradshaws and the facility.

Mrs. Bradshaw's children look at us through suspicious eyes. They still bring cookies and cake, but most of the staff is afraid to eat it. And, as Mrs. Bradshaw grows more demented, her children seem to blame her deteriorating condition on us.

One night, while I was charge, there was a very strange incident.

"Oh my goodness," Martha said, "what time is it? I want to go home right now!"

"Martha," Angie replied, "we just got here; we have another

seven hours to go. Settle down." Angie took a deep breath. "If you help me with my patients tonight, I'll help with yours. I have some extra linen stashed in my locker and we're short a CNA; if we work together and use that system we talked about, we can get done quickly and still have time to watch 'American Idol'.

"Okay" Martha said, the letters dragging out of her mouth like she is about three years old.

They disappeared into the locker room to gather the contraband and then head down the hall with their report sheets in hand.

While the nurses station was quiet, I decided to review my meds and organize my treatments. I've been charge nurse for about three months now and I hate it. The responsibility is more that I can deal with and the staff has sometimes been difficult to manage. They really seem to manage themselves, to the point that I often wonder if I'm just *managing* here in name only.

As I looked over my papers, I heard an awful shrieking sound coming down the hall. I didn't recognize the resident. I immediately looked up at the clock, and noted that it was 3:30 p.m.; and I ran in the direction of the scream.

A resident wasn't shrieking; Martha was.

"Martha, are you all right?" I asked.

Martha stared at a trail of watery stool leading from Mrs. Bradshaw's bed to the bathroom door, which was closed.

I rushed to open the bathroom door and checked to see if Mrs. Bradshaw was all right, but for whatever reason, Martha screamed again. "Martha, will you please be quiet?" I asked her.

"Mrs. Bradshaw," I called through the door, "are you all right? I'm trying to open the door, but I can't because you are leaning against it. Are you Okay?" I gave her a minute, then tried again. "Mrs. Bradshaw, please answer me. Are you all right?"

I turned to look at Martha and noticed that her eyes were still wide. With her hand still covering her mouth, she mumbled something that I couldn't understand. "What did you say, Martha?" I asked her.

Martha took her hand away from her mouth and pointed to Mrs. Bradshaw's cane, which lay on the bed.

"Oh, no," I said. "Her family is going to be so mad."

The reason I said that was because, at the last Care Planning Meeting, Mrs. Bradshaw's family had decided to purchase a lock and key system for her cane. Since that time, we have been supposed to dress her in the morning and place the wristband on her, then attach the cane to the locket on the wristband. There was a treatment order to check the placement every two hours until bedtime. The family had made it clear that they didn't think this was too much to ask for.

"Look," I said to Martha, and then to Angie as well, who had been staring at the situation along with us, "we can't worry about that right now. Help me push the door, so we can see if she's all right."

Mrs. Bradshaw was not answering me as I repeatedly called her name. I was getting more and more anxious as we gently pushed against the door. The entire weight of her body must have been propped against the door. (The door on the other side was locked so that wasn't an option.) Finally, I was able to squeeze through the tiny opening created from all the pushing.

Mrs. Bradshaw was lying there on the floor, trying to talk. Her head was raised off the floor and she looked as if she were going to cry.

I asked her if she was all right, and if anything felt especially painful.

She made a gesture – signaling for a drink.

I called out through the door to Martha and Angie to bring the vital signs equipment, a cup of water, and asked them to please call the nursing supervisor. Then I looked Mrs. Bradshaw over. From an initial physical assessment, she did not appear to have bumped her head or broken any bones, but that was not enough for me. This was an unwitnessed fall and anything could have happened during the event.

I worried about falls among our patients. There was good

reason for this fear; for example, in the past, a patient on the fifth floor fell. The patient had been put back to bed, but her vital signs had become increasingly unstable. The patient had to be transferred to another facility for further management. She died several days later from a subdural hematoma.

The family filed a lawsuit and won. The defendant (the patient's nurse) had to pay $450,000, her nurse's license was suspended for a year, and each time she applies for a job, she has to answer questions about that incident. These things seem to follow you where ever you go. Our nursing judgment is always in question.

Angie brought me a cup of water. I handed it to Mrs. Bradshaw.

She took a sip, cleared her throat and started laughing. "Honey, you would never have guessed what happened. I was walking back from the teachers' lounge and, and, and . . . well, isn't that funny. I don't remember."

I turned to Martha, took the BP cuff from her and began taking Mr. Bradshaw's vital signs.

"OUCH!" Yells Mrs. Bradshaw. "That hurts."

"What hurts, Mrs. Bradshaw?" I asked her.

Mrs. Bradshaw closed her eyes and went limp.

"Quick," I said, "I'll take the vitals while you two call 911 and the nursing supervisor."

Notes:
3:30 p.m. – scream from 321A.

3:31 p.m. – 321A Martha DeSilva CNA and Angie Cromwell CNA present. (+) Trail of watery brown liquid from the bed to the bathroom door, which was closed. Called Mrs. Bradshaw's name 4X, NA (no answer). Unable to open the door, felt like her body was against the door. Other door locked. Called again x 3-4, NA. 3-4 more pushes I was able to get into the bathroom. She was lying on her left side, head against the door, she signaled for me to get her a drink. I asked her to allow me to take her vital signs first. She states she was walking back from the teachers' lounge and then couldn't remember what happened. As I placed the cuff around her arm, she complained of pain, she said "Ouch," when I asked her where it hurt, her eyes closed and her body went limp.

Incident Report
3:30 pm Resident was found on the bathroom floor. There was a trail of brown liquid from her bed to the BR. She stated she was "coming back from the teachers' lounge." Then stated she couldn't remember what happened. V/S 88, 146/82, 24, 98.3. Gene Catalano (phone number), resident's daughter notified, she stated that she will notify the other children. Nursing supervisor – Vicki Giordana, RN, notified, Pager 4532, ambulance dispatched.

Disgruntled family members might be potential plaintiffs. Patients who are interested in having the record reviewed to determine if there were things the healthcare team should have done differently can be potential plaintiffs. According to the documentation, guidelines from CMS, and the policies and procedures of the facilities, the story of what happened and what should have happened from the plaintiff and defense sides will emerge.

Part of the legal process will involve the collection of data relevant to the issues. Besides the medical record, the plaintiff will attempt to recover the incident report. This document belongs to the healthcare facility and it not a part of the medical record, as the medical record is the property of the patient or their designees.

PART 3:
The Legal Side
That Is Serious

Chapter 22
Case Study: Alex Gonzales

Rosale Lobo, RN, MSN, CNS, LNCC
CONFIDENTIAL WORK PRODUCT
TO: X Law Firm
RE: Alex Gonzales

After an extensive review of the medical records presented to me on Alex Gonzales, I find that the nursing care provided during 9/17/06 – 9/28/06 at Chester Medical Center fell below the standards of nursing care. The deviations from the nursing care contributed to Mr. Gonzales' untimely and premature death.

The nurses failed to report signs and symptoms of infection to Dr. Ramish or his designee. Deviations from Mr. Gonzales' baseline vital signs were not reported. The nurses also failed to report signs and symptoms of infection such as elevated temperature, elevated pulse and, on several occasions, below normal blood pressure readings. Mr. Gonzales did not respond to the medication administered for pain in most instances and this was not reported to Dr. Ramish; pain can be considered another sign of infection. There was a consistent assessment described as "constant and throbbing" in the pain category and the nursing staff never reported this to the Orthopedic attending. This is another sign and symptom that is a change in the baseline for any patient and should have been reported to either Dr. Ramish or his designee, Dr. Wright.

According to the Nurse Practice Act, the nurse has a duty to assess for signs and symptoms of diseases and any changes in his or her patient's condition from an established baseline. The nurse is required by law to report findings that deviate from a baseline assessment collected during the patient's episode, then to report any deviated findings to the corresponding physician and wait for further instructions. Follow through on any deviation must be reported in a timely manner to the physician and interventions are delivered according to the physician's orders. The Nurse Practice Act requires that the care and communication of these deviations be documented in the medical record in a contemporaneous manner.

Mr. Gonzales was admitted to the facility on the evening of 9/17/06 after sustaining what the paramedics believed was a right ankle fracture. His vital signs during that time ranged from T 97.6, P 67, R 27, BP 100/61 (Cheyenne Fire and Rescue) to T 97.6, P 69, R 22, BP 94/54 (ER Flow Sheet). These were his baseline vital signs for this hospitalization.

The documentation from the emergency room record states that there were skin changes to his right foot; however, the skin was intact. As described by Dr. Paul Atter on 9/17/06 in the Physical Examination section of his note, "Right lower leg revealed an obvious deformed ankle, which was turned externally. The patient's medial malleolus was tenting the skin with an abrasion over the point of pressure. There is no bone protruding through the skin." This assessment was one of the reasons the physicians decided to repair his fracture without surgery, a closed reduction. Dr. Ramish noted on 9/17/06 that Mr. Gonzales had *poor circulation with PVD.* This was confirmed in the emergency room by the fact that the staff needed the assistance of a Doppler to access a left pedal pulse.

Dr. Ramish considered Mr. Gonzales' medical condition fragile enough to have him admitted for further evaluation of an open reduction internal fixation of his right ankle and Dr. Atter's admitting note states that Mr. Gonzales was *admitted in guarded condition.* Furthermore, an x-ray confirmed placement of the bones on 9/18/06 and the radiologist, Dr. Michael Barnett, was also able to determine that Mr. Gonzales had *extensive arterial calcification.*

Also noted in the documentation for vital sign assessments from 9/19/06 at 8:11 p.m. until the patient was taken into surgery, the pulses ranged from 107-127, and the maximum temperature was 100.2 F. These were signs and symptoms of an infection.

Dr. Ramish was able to repair Mr. Gonzales' fracture in the operating room on 9/21/06.

There was a peri-operative note describing the skin integrity of Mr. Gonzales' right foot. The note stated that the skin is "contaminated". The skin of his right foot is described as having three blisters, all measuring 2-3 cm each. A blister is described as an elevation of the skin containing serous fluid. A dark moist environment is breeding grounds for many infectious agents. The condition of Mr. Gonzales' skin was reported to Dr. Ramish. After the operation, an X-Ray was taken to confirm the repair. Dr. Peter Puller's notes stated "There is a heavy atheromatous vascular calcification present."

Mr. Gonzales was a patient of George Daily, RN, postoperatively, until 7 a.m. on 9/22/09. The post-operative orders written by Dr. Ramish were: HLIV (Hep Lock IV), Morphine 1-4 mg IV Q 1 hour PRN and Percocet 10/325mg PO (By mouth) every 4 hours PRN. These orders are incomplete and should have been questioned by Nurse Daily. When an order is written as "PRN," the prescribing healthcare provider is required to complete the terms with a description for the use of the PRN medication or intervention. In this case, a completed order would have read *PRN for pain.* This nurse further deviated from the standard of care, by not documenting a neurovascular or neuromuscular assessment of the post-operative limb. (8:20 p.m.) There were five sets of V/S taken during shift: Temps were 99.5 -100 (except for one 98.7). Pulse range 100-108. These are all signs and symptoms of an infection. Pain was described as constant and throbbing. There is no documentation that the nurse reported these signs and symptoms to a doctor.

Eric Sauce, RN, received report on Mr. Gonzales from Nurse Daily and was assigned to care for Mr. Gonzales on Friday, 9/22/06, from 7 a.m. – 7 p.m. During this shift, the nurse made three entries describing Mr. Gonzales' pain. Each entry stated that Mr. Gonzales' pain was *constant* and *throbbing.* The nurse did not document that this assessment was reported to Dr. Ramish. When a patient's pain assessment is constant and throbbing for a 12-hour shift, it can be interpreted that the patient is having an unexpected outcome from the surgery and this should be reported to the surgeon. There are no neurovascular or neurological assessments documented. This is a deviation from the standards of nursing care because the patient's primary diagnosis is an Open Reduction Internal Fixation of his right ankle and he has a documented diagnosis of peripheral vascular disease. In addition to this, United Medical Center's Interdisciplinary Plan of Care of the Day was not completed.

Marcus Snow, RN, received a nursing report from Nurse Sauce. Nurse Snow's shift began on Friday, 9/22/06 at 7 p.m. and ended the following morning, Saturday, 9/23/06 at 7 a.m. During this 12-hour shift, Mr. Gonzales' vital sign ranges were T 99.6 – 99.9, P 102-119. The pulse assessments were 30-40 points above his baseline of 67 in the ED and his temperature was two degrees above his baseline. Both were indicative of an infection. There was no documentation that this was reported to Dr. Ramish. Pain during the entire shift was described as *constant* and *throbbing.* The last pain scale for the shift was a zero "0" and the nurse medicated Mr. Gonzales with a Percocet. Nurses are required to administer PRN medication according to the assessment of the patient and his needs. A patient with a pain score of zero does not justify the action to medicate for pain. The documented assessment and intervention did not follow the protocol for pain medication administration. This is a deviation of nursing care standards. Nurse Snow documented a *strong* pedal pulse in the 8:15 p.m. pulse assessment check. This assessment was inconsistent with the physician and emergency department's right pedal pulse assessments.

Anne Kotter, RN, received report from Nurse Snow and was assigned to care for Mr. Gonzales from Saturday, 9/23/06 at 7 a.m. until 7 p.m. that evening. The first documented assessment for pain is at 6:58 a.m. and was described as *constant* and *throbbing* and rated as a "6" there was an intervention of pain medication administration; however, at the two-hour post-pain medication assessment, Ms. Kotter documented that the patient's pain score was a "*4*" and does not offer additional pain medication. As previously noted, Mr. Gonzales was permitted to have up to 4 mg of morphine sulfate every one-hour as needed (for pain). A pain score of "*4*" was not an acceptable goal for this patient and the nurse had orders for pain management. The orders were not followed. This action constitutes a deviation in the standards of nursing care, because a nurse is supposed to be a patient advocate.

The 7:21 a.m. vital sign assessments were outside Mr. Gonzales' baseline; they were 99.8 F, Pulse 114, Blood Pressure 75/33. Diane Marks, the certified nursing assistant, recognized this as a change in condition, and documented that she notified the nurse. Nurse Kotter did not report these abnormal values to the doctor. According to the Nurse Practice Act, nurses are required to report deviations from baselines or any change in condition to the doctor for further orders and interventions. When the Neurovascular Checks are documented, Nurse Kotter stated she assessed a "strong" right pedal pulse, with 1+ slight edema, right foot + 2 moderate and right toes 1+ edema. Given the extent of vascular damage determined by the medical team upon admission into the Emergency Department and the radiologist's report, it would be highly unlikely that this was an accurate assessment.

During the Incision/Wounds assessment, Nurse Kotter described the type of wound as "Incision" that has a dressing that appears *dry-intact*. If the patient's surgical site/area, according to Dr. Ramish's operative note, was dressed with Xeroform, ABD's, Kerlix and a splint, how could the nurse assess the dressing? It was covered under several layers. In fact, the perioperative note of 9/21/06 stated that the dressing consists of all the items in Dr. Ramish's note, plus padding and an Ace wrap. The integrity of this note is questionable. Another questionable assessment occurs at 7:46 a.m. when Nurse Kotter documents a "strong" pedal pulse.

There is a pain assessment at 9:51 a.m. of a "*4*". There is no intervention for Mr. Gonzales. He should have been given the choice of another dose of Morphine or a Percocet tablet. At 11:50 a.m., his pain was described as a 3. Still, there were no interventions for pain management. There is no Plan of the Day completed for Mr. Gonzales, either.

At 12:36 p.m., there were more assessments made on the patient and again Nurse Kotter used the same descriptions for his pedal pulses and edema. The integrity of these assessments is questionable; Mr. Gonzales never had a strong pedal pulse. During this documentation session, the pain score had risen to a 7 with the same "constant" and "throbbing" description, yet the nurse did not administer any medication to help alleviate his pain. In fact, his pain has escalated and there was no intervention to assist with his discomfort.

At 12:36 p.m., there is another pulse assessment to the right pedal and it is described as "strong". At this point, Mr. Gonzales has not been medicated in over five hours. Medication is administered at 12:37 p.m.

At 1:07 pm Diane Marks, the CNA, got another set of vital signs; they were T 103.1, BP 94/40, P 111 and she notified Nurse Kotter. Again, Nurse Kotter did not notify the doctor. Again at 3:43 p.m., Diane Marks informed Nurse Kotter about another elevated temperature of 103.1 and another low BP of 79/37. Was Nurse Kotter deviating from the standard of care by not reporting the abnormal vital signs to the physician? Shouldn't the nurse have double-checked the vital signs? The nurse has a duty to report any signs and symptoms that not only deviate from the patient's baseline, but clearly indicate to a professional nurse that the patient is most likely suffering with an infection. At 4:09 p.m., Mr. Gonzales complained of pain at level "*6*". Again it is characterized as "constant" and "throbbing." Nurse Kotter's intervention – ice, she noted, *unable to medicate at this time.* If the nurse had no orders written that will help the patient achieve an acceptable level of comfort, then, as an advocate for the patient, there should have been a call made to the doctor.

Reporting the effects of an intervention is a nurse's duty. If the prescribed doses are ineffective, the nurse has an obligation to report the findings so the physician can determine if another protocol is required. Nurse Kotter did not medicate Mr. Gonzales at 4:37 p.m., which would have been 4 hours later. At 5:28 p.m. Mr. Gonzales vomited; at 5:35 p.m., Nurse Kotter gave him Percocet 1 tab. One of the side effects of Percocet is nausea; the patient had just vomited, and the nurse should have obtained orders for another route for an analgesic and perhaps an anti-emetic.

Sometime during that morning, Dr. Wright made rounds on Mr. Gonzales. Dr. Wright ordered the IV to be discontinued. Nurse Kotter noted this order at 9:30 a.m. There is no mention in her documentation that the IV has been removed until 5:26 p.m. Since the IV was still in, Nurse Kotter should have used this access to administer the Morphine Sulfate and avoided any further abdominal discomfort to Mr. Gonzales' stomach. Her nursing judgment deviated from the acceptable standards of care.

Nurse Kotter then reported off to Marcus Snow, RN, who was responsible for the patient from Saturday 9/23/06 at 7 p.m. until Sunday, 9/24/06 at 7 a.m. There was one comprehensive assessment done by this nurse for the shift. The Neurovascular Assessment stated that the patient had a "strong" right pedal pulse and the right lower extremity, right toes have +1 edema and the right foot has +2 edema. The pedal pulse, edema and information gathered from previous notes within this record deems this assessment inconsistent with the patient's presentation.

There were three sets of vital signs recorded during this shift: (6:56 p.m. - T 99.2F, P 105, BP 73/34; 12:30 a.m. – T 99.4F, P 120, BP 82/40 and 3:37 a.m. - T 99.4F, P 111, BP 78/40); there is no documentation from Mark Howard, CNA, that the nurse was notified. Mr. Howard deviated from the standards of care.

Nurse Snow gave report to Cathy Hertz, LPN. Cathy Hertz, LPN, was working under Anne Kotter, RN, in the care of Mr.

Gonzales from Sunday, 9/24/06 at 7 a.m. until Sunday 9/24/06 at 7 p.m. The vital signs recorded at 7:21 a.m. state T 100.3 F, P 131, R 20. Diane Marks noted that the nurse was notified, but Nurse Kotter did not notify Drs. Wright or Ramish that the patient was exhibiting signs of an infection. Also at 7:30 a.m. in the documentation, Nurse Hertz states in her Respiratory assessment that the patient has *tachypnea*. This implies a rapid respiratory rate (although it was documented as *"20"*), another symptom that should have been reported to the physician.

There was a comprehensive Neurovascular assessment at 7:30 a.m. This was the first mention of a complaint to Mr. Gonzales' right foot assessment of *numbness and tingling*, another change of condition that should have been reported to the surgeon. At that same time, there is a pulse assessment of the pedal pulse: *strong*, a complaint of *calf tenderness to the right leg with movement* and the nurse under the right pedal pulse assessment states *inaccessible.* The numerous deviations in assessments and the lack of communication to the physicians constitute deviations in the nursing care provided by this nurse. At 7:30 a.m., Mr. Gonzales complained of nausea; by 8:15 a.m., he vomited, and then again at 10:20 a.m. None of these symptoms were reported to the physician, which is another deviation in the standard of care. The vital signs recorded at 12:39 p.m., T 99.7, P 117, were taken by the nursing assistant, who documented that she reported it to the nurse, but according to the documentation, these important assessment values were never reported to the physician. At 3:00 p.m. in Nurse Hertz's documentation, she describes Mr. Gonzales' right ankle feeling as *constant* and *aching.* At 3:36 p.m. Mr. Gonzales has a pulse of 111, clearly a sign of an infectious process in his body.

Nurse Hertz reported off to Andy Brown, RN, who was responsible for the care of Mr. Gonzales from 9/24/06 from 7 p.m. until 9/25/06 at 7 a.m.

There are entries made about Mr. Gonzales' neurological status that are all outside of his neurological baseline. Nurse

Brown's shift began one hour before this assessment was documented. The words she used to describe Mr. Gonzales' neurological status are: confused, *drowsy, disoriented* and *hard to wake*. There was no call to the physician and there was not another assessment of his neurological status for the remainder of this shift. Clearly, this is a symptom of an infection and a deviation in the nursing care standards.

There are discrepancies in the assessment of the extremities that also demonstrate inconsistent and questionable integrity. *Numbness* and *tingling* were described as Mr. Gonzales' sensation to the right foot. This is an abnormal finding and was not reported. The nurse described the pedal pulse as *strong*, yet *inaccessible*. There are obvious flaws in the documentation that deem these entries suspicious.

Mr. Gonzales entered the hospital via ambulance because he slipped in the bathroom and injured his right ankle. It was determined that it was a closed fracture; however, there is documentation stating that there was tenting to his skin at the sight of the fracture, his pedal pulses could only be obtained with a Doppler in the emergency room and then the radiology report stated that Mr. Gonzales has extensive arterial calcification. He was then admitted under guarded condition. During his operative stay, the nurse noted that Mr. Gonzales' skin was contaminated with three blisters. Dr. Ramish was aware of Mr. Gonzales' skin disposition, but there were no provisional orders made for this patient, who had Peripheral Vascular Disease and contaminated skin changes.

The nursing care following the surgery clearly shows deviation in nursing care standards. Even if the nurses caring for the patient were not aware of the disposition of the covered skin, they had an obligation to report anything that is abnormal. They had an obligation to assess for signs and symptoms of changes in the patient and specific assessments based on the patient's diagnoses: the right ankle fracture, open reduction infernal fixation and peripheral vascular disease. The nurses assessed abnormal vital signs, changes in Mr. Gonzales physical presentation, neurological presentation, and pain control or lack thereof, but none of these aspects were reported to Dr. Ramish.

There are documented assessments that state Mr. Gonzales had strong pedal pulses, but the pictures of his skin after the dressing was removed demonstrate that a manual pedal pulse assessment would have been very unlikely. The words used to describe the kind of pain, "aching" and "constant," are used at least 15 times in the assessments. Not one of the nurses documented that they reported this to Dr. Ramish or his designee.

All of these poor actions in nursing judgment contributed to Mr. Gonzales' advanced septic condition, change in level of consciousness, and his premature death.

Chapter 23

Deposition of George Daily, RN
Taken by the Plaintiff

Appearances

For the Plaintiff:	*Attorney: Robert Smith*
For the Defendant:	*Attorney: Karen Duffy*
Dr. Ramish	
For the Defendant:	*Attorney: Darlene Friedland*
Chester Medical Center	

(Below is an excerpt of the deposition already in progress)

Q. Would you state your full name?

A. George. The last name is Daily.

Q. And would you spell your first name?

A. G-E-O-R-G-E.

Q. Mr. Daily, are you a registered nurse?

A. I am.

Q. Can you give me a little information about your educational background?

A. I graduated from Baker County Community College.

Q. What degree did you get from Baker Community County College?

A. An associate's degree in nursing.

Q. And where is Baker County?

A. It is in Somewhere, USA.

Q. Then what is your further education after that?

A. That is my education. I mean, I didn't go beyond that. I didn't get a BSN.

Q. You're licensed to practice nursing in this state?

A. Yes, sir.

Q. When did you become licensed to do that?

A. In October of 2000.

Q. Your associate degree in nursing qualified you to become a registered nurse, then?

A. Yes, sir.

Q. Did you do testing to be certified as a registered nurse?

A. In Anywhere, USA is where I took the test.

Q. All right. Okay. So you're licensed in Here, USA as well?

A. As well, yes, sir.

Q. Is that active and current?

A. It is.

Q. And you've stayed active and currently licensed as a registered nurse since October of 2000?

A. Yes, sir.

Q. I noticed, I think, in some materials that were given to me by the hospital that you began employment at the hospital in December of 2000?

A. December 4th.

Q. And you've been continuously employed there since?

A. Yes, sir.

Q. Do you have any area of nursing that you focus on, a specialty?

A. I'm in the resource pool. So I work in all areas of the hospital.

Q. And what areas of nursing have you worked in while employed at the hospital?

A. In ICU, ER, ortho, neuro, oncology, med/surg, surgical.

Q. The case that we're here about is the Alex Gonzales matter. He died at the hospital. Do you remember Mr. Gonzales?

A. No, sir, I don't.

Q. I'm the attorney for his family. His wife is Mary and some of the other family members. So I'm sure your attorney, the attorney for the hospital, has told you that I'm going to ask you questions about Mr. Gonzales. It's significant to me that you don't remember this patient, huh?

A. No, sir, I don't.

Q. Have you had a chance to look at any of the medical records that pertain to Mr. Gonzales?

A. Yes.

Q. Did you find in those records that you did provide care to him?

A. Yes.

Q. What records did you review?

A. His chart, the full chart.

Q. What's in front of us here is a notebook that says Exhibit 3 on it. It's blue. And it's the entire medical record that the hospital has provided Mr. Gonzales. Did you review all of those documents? You can look through it, if you'd like. Take your time and look through it and be familiar with it. Let me know when you are ready and I will ask you a question.

A. Okay. I think I'm ready. These are the ones that I looked at.

Q. And one in particular in that blue notebook you were just looking through, what part of it?

A. Just where I'd been – my initials showed up, the date that I had Mr. Gonzales.

Q. And at the top of – would you give us the page number? In the bottom right-hand corner, there's a page number? Can you read that?

A. It looks like 176.

Q. Three zeros and 176?

A. Three zeros and 176.

Q. And there's an MRP number over to the left of that.

A. That's 0178.

Q. And at the top of that sheet, it says Discharge A, doesn't it?

A. Yes, sir.

Q. And those were the materials you just spent some time looking through to refresh your recollection, I think, about your care for Mr. Gonzales?

A. Yes, sir.

Q. But as I understand, you've also seen these previous to just right now, then?

A. Yes.

Q. Are you – have you seen medical records that have been printed out as they are in this Discharge A before?

A. No, I have not.

Q. What form are you used to seeing the medical records in?

A. Well, I'm not sure I understand the question. I don't ever see medical records once they leave the floor. I see them in the chart form where the doctor's orders are and then like radiology and cardiopulmonary in separation, but that's – I've never seen this format before until now.

Q. The format that you described for that page that gave the Discharge A does not appear in the form in the written chart. In the physical chart, then, does it?

A. No.

Q. Did you find from your review of the records that you provided care to Mr. Gonzales in September of 2006?

A. According to these initials, yes, I did.

Q. And were you working on the ortho floor, the orthopedic floor, at the time?

A. That night, yes. Again, I'm resource. I go to different floors different nights.

Q. I see. I didn't know what that quite meant. That means that you kind of float around. I don't know if that's the right word or not.

A. Yes, it is the right word. I do float around.

Q. Where needed?

A. Where needed. PRN, yes.

Q. Correct. So you, in September 2006, then, you were not assigned specifically to the orthopedic floor; is that right?

A. No, sir.

Q. But that night you were.

A. Yes, sir.

Q. Where in 2006, where was the orthopedic floor? Where was it located in the hospital?

A. It would be on the fourth floor.

Q. And you mentioned in the answer to my question that you had worked ortho/neuro. I thought you kind of put those two words together?

A. It's an ortho/neuro floor. It takes care of orthopedics as well as neurologic.

Q. And what kind of patients would be on that floor for neurologic?

A. Oh, like back surgeries, head surgeries, something like that involves neurology.

Q. The neurosurgeons?

A. Neurosurgeons have patients there, uh-hum.

Q. How many beds for orthopedic and neuro were there in September 2006 on the fourth floor?

A. I believe 24.

Q. Because I know you don't recall, let me tell you about the time period. 17 September was the date of hospitalization and admission, of 2006, a Sunday, and Mr. Gonzales passes away on the 27th of September, 2006, about a ten-day period of time in there.

Now, my understanding is you don't recall this patient during that period of time. What I'd like to ask you is just generally, then, during that period of time, how did you receive your assignments?

A. I come on at 7:00 p.m. and I'm given a list of patients by the charge nurse.

Q. Where do you go to get your assignment? Where did you go at that time to get your assignment?

A. I don't know specifically where I got my assignment that night, but it could be in the report room. It could be at the nurses' station, wherever I happened to run into the charge nurse when I get there.

Q. And the charge nurse. Is there just one charge nurse for the entire hospital per shift?

A. For that floor, for that shift.

Q. Okay. So this would have been the charge nurse for ortho/neuro?

A. Yes, sir.

Q. How did you know to go to ortho/neuro that night?

A. The staffing office tells me where to go.

Q. How far in advance do they tell you that?

A. When I get there.

Q. And it looked to me from my review of these same records that you were caring for Mr. Gonzales just one evening and it was the evening of the 21st of September starting – the first entry I see is at 8:20 in the evening.

A. Yes, sir.

Q. And then through that night until 6:08 in the morning?

A. It would go beyond a little, about 7:00.

Q. That was a typical shift – in terms of period of time, that was a typical shift for you?

A. Yes, sir.

Q. When you reviewed the records, either just now or previous to now, did you – could you tell what kind of a patient Mr. Gonzales was; in other words, what his medical problems were?

A. Not from the moment I got him, but as the night wore on, I would assume that I would sit down and try and read his chart to see if there were past history.

Q. Why don't we just approach it that way, then. You were assigned to Mr. Gonzales for the evening shift the 21st of September, going into the morning hours of the 22nd.

A. Yes, sir.

Q. Based upon your habit and practice, how would you have approached his care?

A. Once I received report from the PACU that he's coming over, then I just set up the room. Knowing that it's a male patient, set it up for a male patient. Once the patient arrives, then I go in and make a quick assessment, and then after he's settled in, then do a complete assessment.

Q. PACU is post anesthesia care unit?

A. Yes, sir.

Q. So you would have known that he came out of surgery?

A. Yes, sir.

Q. Do you believe you were the first nurse to care for Mr. Gonzales post-surgery?

A. I believe so.

Q. What did your quick assessment – or what would your quick assessment have included at that time?

A. Just to see about his orientation; just, you know, introduce myself to him; just to make sure that he's good and alert.

Q. Would you document that?

A. Not necessarily. I would later, I think, in his neuro assessment.

Q. You said you would get him settled in. I assume that to mean you would have gotten him into bed?

A. Right.

Q. Then you would have done, I think you said, a –

A. Complete assessment.

Q. Complete assessment. What could your complete assessment have entailed?

A. I would begin with him neurologically again and then his respiratory status. Then I would go right down the line that we have on our computer. I can't give you the exact line, but it entails gastrointestinal, musculoskeletal, renal, reproductive. Psychosocial would be the final.

Q. In the Discharge A forms, did you find – or can you find at 8:30 that you actually did document an assessment?

A. What I'm looking at is the neurovascular check at 8:20.

Q. I'd like to ask you some questions about the neurovascular check.

A. Okay.

Q. Under sensation, do you see under Generalized, you put "present"?

A. Yes.

Q. Why did you make that indication or that note?

A. That he can feel, touch; that he has sensation in his skin; that he can feel in different places in this body.

Q. When it says generalized, that would be where anatomically? Where in the body would you have been feeling?

A. Shoulders, arms, legs, feet.

Q. Generally, the person has sensation, then?

A. Yes. And if he doesn't feel it, then he would indicate that.

Q. And under the right foot, you have, "numbness, tingling." Am I right?

A. No.

Q. Okay. What did you have under –

A. Mine is blank.

Q. Sensation?

A. Yes.

Q. You don't believe that you would have assessed his sensation in the right foot at that time?

A. Yes, I believe that I would have.

Q. Would there not be some note there if you had done that?

A. I didn't make a note, but in my general standard of care, I would do that.

Q. If there's nothing written there, what does that mean?

A. I simply did not chart it or did not find any numbness and/or tingling.

Q. I looked at some material that was provided to me by the hospital and my sense of Care Manager was that if the nurse did an assessment within – and the findings were within normal limits – and I may have this wrong – that they did not document. They only documented exceptions to the normal limits.

A. Yes.

Q. Is that your understanding?

A. Yes.

Q. Would that mean that under Sensation for the right foot, then you found it to have normal sensation? Is that how one would interpret a blank?

A. I did not – he did not – the patient did not indicate any numbness and/or tingling to me. That would be my assumption.

Q. And under color – it's on the next page, 177.

A. Okay.

Q. What entry did you make?

A. Appropriate for race.

Q. Generalized, correct?

A. Generalized.

Q. Which would be again the entire body?

A. Yes, sir.

Q. What about color for right toe?

A. It's blank. I didn't document anything.

Q. That could mean that it wasn't assessed, then?

A. It could, but I doubt it. Generally, that's my – I assess everything. If there is no exception, then I would not document to my – the way I would assess.

Q. And temperature?

A. Is warm. I documented generalized, warm.

Q. Again, that would be the whole body, correct?

A. Yes, sir.

Q. Nothing, no indication for right toes?

A. No, sir.

Q. And under Edema Assessment, do you find that?

A. Yes, sir.

Q. And for the right foot, what is there?

A. Slight edema.

Q. What does that mean? What picture would one get in their mind?

A. What little I could see of the foot – and I'm assuming that it was dressed from the surgery – I could see slight edema, swelling.

Q. Where would you look to see that?

A. Probably in the toes would be the open area that I would see.

Q. And how does a nurse assess between slight and any other scale of edema?

A. That's a judgment from slight to moderate to, you know deep. I could just – I'm assuming I could just see slight puffiness, and I would assume, you know, that I would assess it to other toes that I've seen.

Q. There's an entry on – I think it's one 0183 for neuro checks. Do you see that?

A. Uh-hum?

Q. And at the bottom, it has the Glasgow scale, consciousness scale?

A. Uh-hum.

Q. 15. Then does it say, "Vitals done"?

A. Uh-hum.

Q. And it says, "yes"?

A. Uh-hum.

Q. One thing I need to tell you is you need to answer verbally without saying uh-huhs because the court reporter won't get it down right.

A. I'm sorry.

Q. But it says, "Yes, vitals done."

A. Yes.

Q. When were they done?

A. The first set of vitals that I see were taken at what looks like 2145 on page 00104.

Q. I'm looking at that page and it doesn't appear to have your signature. Why do you believe that is your –

A. That is not mine. That's the CNA.

Q. When you're assigned as an RN, for example, to the ortho floor —?

A. Yes, sir.

Q. —then the floor also has CNAs that work there as well?

A. Yes, sir.

Q. Do they work under you?

A. They work with me.

Q. Had you worked with this CNA before?

A. I'm sorry, I don't recall –

Q. Okay.

A. — her specifically.

Q. Do you – when you get on your floor, you ask her to do that?

A. Yes.

Q. You would ask her to take vital signs?

A. Yes, sir.

Q. Are you supposed to co-sign for the CNA for vital signs?

A. I don't know whether we're supposed to co-sign for vital signs for CNAs.

Q. Are you supposed to co-sign in any capacity for the CNA's documentation?

A. I think we did a long time ago and then it kind of went away, but I can't answer that specifically.

Q. Your recollection today is at 2145 on the 21st of September, the CNA did vital signs for this patient under your registered nurse care?

A. Yes. Sir.

Q. And then the next one, I think, is at 2300 on the next page, 105.

Silence

Q. Actually, they go on.

A. Oh, that's right. She does.

Q. And then all the entries after that would have been your – you're actually doing the work, then.

A. Yes, sir.

Q. What was your understanding of how often during a shift you should do the neurovascular check in September 2006?

A. I do the assessment — originally the neurovascular checks. I do them periodically through the night, unless there is a specific order to do them at a specific time, then I just do them routinely on my own. The vital signs I do under direction of the post-operative vital signs.

Q. The direction that a registered nurse gets come from post-surgery?

A. I'm not sure I understand.

Q. How do you know – you've been assigned this patient?

A. Yes, sir.

Q. You're a registered nurse. How do you know what to do to care for this patient? I would understand that you do your own assessment. Do you get guidance from the doctor?

A. Well, okay. I would look at the orders, the transfer orders from the PACU to the floor to see if there was anything specific that would be outside what I would normally do.

Q. You described to me before what you would normally do –

A. Yes.

Q —in terms of getting the patient in, do a quick assessment and then a complete assessment.

A. Yes, sir.

Q. What did you – are you able to tell me from the records you reviewed what orders you did get?

A. They go back to the doctor's orders. Page 38, yes, that's the one.

Q. Is that the one? We've had Dr. Ramish testify about that. We know it says by his reading. What in that is important to you or gave you any specific direction as the receiving registered nurse on the floor?

A. All right. Would you repeat the question, please?

Q. Right. What did you take from this order as being specific instructions to you in the caring of Mr. Gonzales?

A. I do not see anything that would be specific. These are routine orders to me. It's his medication list, his diet, what to do with the IV site. The only thing outstanding that I would say would be a little different would be the one medication, to be held if a heart rate were less than 60 or SBP – or less than 100.

Q. What, if anything would that alert you to?

A. Just to watch his blood pressure, watch his heart rate.

Q Do you know whether Dr. Ramish at that time had any standing orders for this ortho patients' coming out of surgery?

A. I don't know.

Q. Would they probably be in the chart if he did have them?

A. Not necessarily. They could be on the unit somewhere, but I don't recall.

Q. This order does not have any indications about your role in taking care of the wound, does it?

A. No,

Q. And the absence of that, what did that tell you in terms of your care of this patient?

A. Again, I'm not sure I understand.

Q. From this order and the absence of an order regarding that wound, what was your plan or intention in terms of taking care of this patient and his surgical wound?

A. To monitor, to see if there would be bleeding of any kind; if there were, to reinforce that dressing. To see if there were acute changes of swelling, you know, would be –

Q. Color as well?

A. Color possibly, yes.

Q. We're talking about the color of the toes?

A. Yes.

Q. Have you received orthopedic patients post-surgery where you have been asked to treat the wound?

A. I never have. The physicians generally do not like you to address their dressings or do anything with their dressings until at least 24 hours post-op. Only if there is excess bleeding to reinforce.

Q. What about after 24 hours post-op?

A. Generally, the surgeon has come in and changed the dressing and then he sometimes will write specific orders.

Q. Was it your understanding then, in September of 2006, that if there was no direction in the doctor's orders that you should not change the dressing yourself?

A. I would not, no.

Q. Have you received orders from doctors after the 24 hour period to change the dressing yourself? And when you have received that order, what words have the doctor used to give you that message?

A. I'm sorry, would you repeat?

Q. Yes. On those occasions when you have received orders after the 24 hours to care for the wound, what words do they use to tell you that you should do that?

A. Wound care generally comes in and does their assessment. The doctor might write to change the dressing every four days or PRN. I mean, it's very broad. That's not always the case, but I mean they're very broad.

Q. When you saw wound care would come in, what do you mean by that?

A. That's the wound care department. They generally are consulted.

Q. For after the 24 hours in an orthopedic patient?

A. Yes, sir.

Q. And that would be, I suppose, the reason that you don't do much of the wound care because there's a special department that does that?

A. Generally speaking, that's true.

Q. And generally, they are involved with the orthopedic patients after the 24 hours? I'll clear that up, we're talking about that time period of 17 to 27 September, 2006.

A. Okay. Then – okay. You need to repeat where they were.

Q. Generally in that time period, orthopedic patients for post-surgery, after 24 hours, it's been your observation that wound care comes in and takes care of the wounds. If you can remember, go ahead.

A. Wound care would generally be consulted 24 hours after. That is not always the case. The doctor may write specific orders to dress or re-dress that wound. That is not always the case. If I see a soiled dressing post 24 hours and, you know, there are no specific orders, I might change it, depending on how soiled and/or how stained it might be, but usually by then, the physician has been there and has checked his dressing that he did in surgery and has either changed it or has left orders what to do for it.

Q. Your 8:20 assessment included a nursing pain assessment. Did you find that in the records? You might try 0233. At 8:20, did you do a nursing pain assessment?

A. I did.

Q. And you assessed the pain at 8?

A. I did.

Q. What was your understanding in 2006 of how often you were to assess the pain for a post-surgical patient?

A. Would you repeat?

Q. Yeah. In September of 2006, what was your understanding of how often, the frequency that you were to assess the patient's pain?

A. Every two hours.

Q. And do you have anything in writing that guides you on the periodic nature, the frequency with which you are supposed to do certain assessments? Did you in 2006?

A. Do you mean there are written instructions to that effect?

Q. I'm sorry, what I'm really asking is did you personally – how did you personally know the different frequencies that you were supposed to do the various assessments?

A. From the guidelines from the hospital, from administration.

Q. And are those in writing?

A. I don't know.

Q. Do you personally carry a notebook or any other way to remind yourself of that or did you in September 2006?

A. No. That's just my standard and based on hospital policy that I've been told we need to assess pain levels every two hours.

Q. For post-surgical patients?

A. For all patients.

Q. Now, there's a designation in the Discharge A for – I think it's SDS pain as well as nursing pain. Do you recall that? Do you know that?

A. No.

Q. Okay. That doesn't strike a familiarity with you as to SDS pain?

A. No.

Q. Okay. Now, it looked from what I saw that you assessed pain at 8:20 and then again around six o'clock in the morning. But now that I know there is a CNA involved, maybe she did some assessments as well or can you look in the records and see if that's true?

A. Would you repeat again, please?

Q. Yeah. It looks to me like you did a nursing pain assessment on this patient at 8:20 in the evening and again at six o'clock in the morning.

A. No.

Q. Okay. What else did you do?

A. At ten o'clock, at midnight, at 2:00, at 2302 and 04 and again 06.

Q. What pages are you looking at?

A. At 233.

Q. I see the assessment at 8:20, 2020 written on page 0233 and I don't –

A. Drop straight down.

Q. Okay, where do I go?

A. It's right below this top part here.

Q. I see that.

A. And the next block shows 9-1, then into 9-22.

Q. Correct.

A. And you'll see my assessment at ten o'clock, 2200, then again at midnight, then 0202.

Q. Correct.

A. And 0400. And then again on the next page at 0600.

Q. Those are WNL.

A. All within normal limits.

Q. Now, for pain, what does that communicate to the next nurse or physician?

A. That he has been pain free.

Q. So on a scale of 1 to 10 that would be equivalent of a zero?

A. Yes.

Q. How did you in September of 2006 probably for this patient assess pain?

A. If he's awake, I would ask. If he's asleep, I would just look at his respirations, whether I see any distress. If he is sleeping, I would not bother him, because generally speaking, a person in pain is awake and will tell you that they're in pain and then I would address it.

Q. Do you know whether the patient was medicated at that time?

A. Where he was medicated?

Q. Whether?

A. Not at those times that are within normal limits, no. Back up at 8:20, if you look down the column, you'll see that I medicated him at that time.

Q. And you gave 2 milligrams of morphine?

A. Yes, sir.

Q. How long would that have affected his pain?

A. I can't answer that truthfully because different people respond differently.

Q. I guess what I'm wondering, in your assessment, was he without pain these various hours beginning really at actually 2050 and then throughout the evening until at least four o'clock?

A. Yes, sir.

Q. Was he without pain because of the medication or because he was pain free or do you know?

A. I don't know. I can't answer that.

Q. But your assessment is of this individual, he was pain free for those – when you indicate WNL, within normal limits?

A. That he was not complaining of pain at those times.

Q. Is there a way to note if the patient is asleep during that assessment in this record?

A. If it's charted that way – you know, if I would chart that he's sleeping, would be the only way that I know of.

Q. And because you did not chart that he was sleeping, would you reasonably communicate that he probably verbalized to you that he had no pain?

A. Yes. That or he just was resting quietly. I didn't bother him and just went on.

Q. Thank you for that clarification. Now, that's the only entries I have for 8:20 assessment. Was that your complete assessment that you did of Mr. Gonzales?

A. Yes, sir.

Q. With respect to everything. What I have, Mr. Daily. He had a neurovascular check, a neuro check and a nursing pain check at 8:20. Does that sound like what you would do for a complete assessment?

A. Yes, sir. Again, I would add in others, gastrointestinal, musculoskeletal; I go through the whole column.

Q. And you believe you would have done that on this case?

A. I believe so.

Q. Let's look at the vitals, if you can find that section. They begin numbers 000 – lots of zeros, 95. And please give the MRP number as well.

A. I got it.

Q. Let's kind of track the temperatures with me, if you would then. 99.5 at 9:45 on the 21st of September, then 99.5, 99.3. Would you consider those to be within normal parameters for a post-op patient?

A. I would.

Q. And then the next page, 105, 99.5 again, which you believe would be normal, and 97.7 at 2300, correct?

A. Uh-hum. Yes.

Q. 97.7 is a dip in temperature, correct?

A. Yes, sir.

Q. Does that alert you as a registered nurse or would it to anything?

A. No, it would not.

Q. Within normal limits?

A. Yes, sir.

Q. Now, at 2330, there is no – nothing written there. Would a reader of this, then, take it to mean that the temperature was not taken?

A. Yes, sir.

Q. What was your understanding in 2006, September, how often temperature should be taken in a patient like Mr. Gonzales?

A. I can't – I don't know that specifically. Once I look it over the vital signs at 97.7, that's a normal temperature for me. If I don't see any visible changes, I might not take a temperature again. If you go to page 106, you will see that I did, in fact start to take a temperature again.

Q. How did you take – would you probably have taken the temperature in September of 2006?

A. By tympanic.

Q. And what does that mean?

A. That means out of the ear.

Q. An instrument that –

A. Goes in the ear.

Q. And so we see on page 106, then at 98.7, 99 and at three o'clock 99.3, all within your experience and judgment within normal limits?

A. Within my judgment of post-op surgeries, yes.

Q. The last temperature, then, I have is at 6:08 and that was a hundred degrees Fahrenheit. Do you see that?

A. Yes, sir.

Q. How did you feel about that temperature? How would you have felt about that temperature?

A. Again, I would not be alarmed. That's a normal body response to surgery.

Q. Still within 24 hours of surgery?

A. Yes. Yes, sir.

Q. I want to go back to your early experience with a patient like Mr. Gonzales. You're given the assignment. You come on the floor. I understand now the complete assessment that you did. But you would probably try to make yourself familiar with this gentleman through other people's writing and documentation, correct?

A. I'm not sure I understand. Are you asking me would I be looking at other people's charting?

Q. Yeah, charting on this patient, yes. Would you review anybody else's charting, any other documentation that preceded your experience with them?

A. Not necessarily, because I received him post-surgically. So my assessment is probably going to be somewhat different than prior to.

Q. Is it important to you as a registered nurse, taking a patient out of post-op, that you do a complete assessment of him?

A. Yes, sir.

Q. Why is that?

A. Well, just to see what his status is. I'm not sure I understand, but I assess all patients equally, the same way, not just a post-op patient.

Q. Would it be important to you to know the patient's previous medical history?

A. Not at the moment I receive him, but then I would like to know about it later through the course of the night, given the opportunity to read the chart.

Q. And how would you do that? How would you get to know his previous medical history?

A. Just by looking at the history and H&P, looking at previous doctors' orders, looking at doctors' progress notes, those types of ways.

Q. When you say looking at, do I imagine you're looking at a hard copy of the actual chart itself?

A. Yes, sir.

Q. What about – do you go into the computer and look at previous documentation on this patient that is in the computer?

A. By other RNs and/or other staff you're talking about?

Q. Correct.

A. Not always. Sometimes.

Q. And you don't recall whether you did on this patient or not?

A. No, sir, I don't.

Q, But you would think, though, you would have gone through the chart to know what was ever in the chart on this particular shift to know that you had?

A Not shift-related, but just historical. I'm missing your question, I guess.

Q. Sure. During your shift sometime, you probably would have gone to the chart and read what was in it?

A. Yes, sir, if I had time.

Q. And you don't know whether you did or not with this patient, correct?

A. I can't answer that truthfully, no.

Q. Is it common that you usually have more than one patient when you're on the orthopedic/neuro floor?

A. Yes, sir.

Q. And you probably would have this night as well?

A. I'm sorry.

Q. You probably would during this particular night as well have more than one patient?

A. Yes, sir.

Chapter 24
Deposition of Eric Snow, RN
Taken by the Plaintiff
Appearances

For the Plaintiff: Attorney: Robert Smith

For the Defendant: Attorney: Karen Duffy
Dr. Ramish

For the Defendant: Attorney: Darlene Friedland
Chester Medical Center

(This is an excerpt of the deposition already in progress)

Q. Okay. Now, for the care – have you had a chance to look through the medical records some to kind of refresh your memory about the care of Mr. Gonzales?

A. Yes.

Q. You told us you remembered some things about him, just about his multiple co-morbidities and he was Hispanic. Do you recall anything else about the gentleman or his care or about him?

A. Not specifically.

Q. Did you know his – did you get to meet his family?

A. Yes.

Q. Do you remember the family?

A. Not really.

Q. You just remember that there was family.

A. Yes. His wife was with him most of the time.

Q. Did you probably see her, then, in the room or on the floor where he was being hospitalized?

A. Yes.

Q. Other family members as well came to visit, or do you recall?

A. I don't recall.

Q. But his wife in particular you do remember?

A. Yes.

Q. What about her do you remember? For example, do you remember any conversations with her or just how she was as a person?

A. No.

Q. By example only, some of the visitors at a hospital can be known to the nursing staff to be an annoyance, to be demanding, or to be nice and pleasant. Do you recall what she was on a scale like that?

A. No.

Q. Okay. You saw – let me back up for a minute. Based on your review of the records, did you see that you saw Mr. Gonzales on Friday, the 22nd, during the day?

A. Yes.

Q. Is there anything that stands out in your mind about the care that you provided on the 22nd?

A. No.

Q. No events that you thought were remarkable from your experience and training on the 22nd?

A. No.

Q. You knew that he was post-surgery on that day. You recall that from your records that he had his surgery done?

A. Yes.

Q. It actually was done on the 21st, on a Thursday. Okay. There's an entry at page 224. If you want to look in the bottom right hand corner, it has those numbers. It's a nursing I-N-C, slash, wound. Do you see that?

A. Yes.

Q. It looks like at 7:45 that morning you did an assessment of the wounds.

A. Yes.

Q. What do you do when you do your assessment to complete that part of the computer documentation? Let me ask that differently. Do you recall what you did at 7:45 with Mr. Gonzales?

A. A wound assessment depends on the wound and the circumstances. With Mr. Gonzales, his wound was wrapped in a soft cast. So I would have felt for his pedal pulse, checked his capillary refill, noted if there was any odor from the cast and made sure that the dressing is intact, that it's not impaired in any way.

Q. And you could – with your hand, you could feel a pedal pulse?

A. Yeah. You had to put two fingers under the wrap to feel it, but, yes.

Q. You think you probably did that?

A. Yes.

Q. Do you remember specifically doing that? Do you have an independent memory of doing that?

A. On the 25th, yes.

Q. Okay. We'll get there. On the 22nd, no, I would take it.

A. It was my habit to do that. So I would say yes.

Q. Okay, Under Wound Appearance, you – what is entered on the computer is "unable to see." Do you know why that is there?

A. The incision was covered with a bandage.

Q. Have you, as a registered nurse, unwrapped bandages for fractured ankles?

A. It depends what the bandage is.

Q. Tell me more about that.

A. If it's splinted in what is considered a soft cast, the nurse does not remove that. If the wound, however, is only wrapped just to keep it covered and keep it clean, we do change those bandages.

Q. Does it depend on what the doctor orders are?

A. Sometimes.

Q. How so? Would you explain that?

A. Nurses do not change the bandage unless it's been ordered by the physician.

Q. Was that also true in September 2006?

A. Yes.

Q. Okay. And that would be true – would have been true with respect to Mr. Gonzales' splint or dressing?

A. Yes.

Q. So when you say "Unable to see," I guess I assume that's because the wrapping prevented you from seeing the appearance of the incision?

A. Yes.

Q. Did you at that time, using your nursing judgment, see any reason to remove the wrap?

A. No.

Q. You would have looked for that, wouldn't you? As a registered nurse?

A. Yes.

Q. This was the first – this on the 22nd was the first time you had known Mr. Gonzales?

A. Yes.

Q. What was your – what did you do to become familiar with Mr. Gonzales, to know how you would proceed with your nursing care that day?

A. A couple of things. I would have gotten report from the off-going nurse, which would tell me his needs and his abilities.

Q. His what?

A. Needs.

Q. I'm sorry?

A. Needs.

Q. Needs. Thank you.

A. I also could review his chart.

Q. Is that probable what you did review his chart?

A. It was my habit, yes.

Q. Is that what's called a paper chart?

A. Both are kept on the floor. The electronic record the nurses have access to in a computer and a hard copy of the chart is kept on the floor.

Q. Was it your review of those materials that let you know he had multiple co-morbidities?

A. Yes.

Q. And what as a – what did that mean to you with respect to Mr. Gonzales in terms of how you would be caring for him that day?

A. Knowing the history of alcohol abuse meant that I would watch for signs of withdrawal. Knowing that he had peripheral vascular disease meant that I needed to assess his pulses and the temperature of his extremities. And knowing that he was in kidney failure meant that I would watch for his level of consciousness, watch for his reaction to medication, as well as the fractured ankle, watching for anything to go wrong with that.

Q. Before we leave the 22nd, then, what would you want to note about the temperature of his foot?

A. If it's normal or not. When watching vital signs, temperature-wise after surgery, we want to know if they have a fever, if their temperature is too low or if it's normal.

Q. If there's fever, what does that – what would that have told you?

A. Depends on the circumstances.

Q. Well under the circumstances of Mr. Gonzales, if he developed a fever during your watch?

A. It depends – what was going on at the time. If he were, you know, being physically active or under too many blankets, that could raise his temperature, and it would depend how high the temperature is as to if it would be significant or not.

Q. Let's go to the date Monday, which is the 25th of September. You recall independently that you did see him again after the 22nd?

A. Yes.

Q. Tell us, do you remember any changes that you saw in Mr. Gonzales when you saw him on the 25th?

A. I remember that his level of consciousness was altered compared to when I cared for him on the 22nd.

Q. Altered in what way?

A. He was very confused, stuporous even, more lethargic than he had been.

Q. And as a nurse with your background and experience, what did that – how did you – what did you think about that?

A. With his co-morbidities, it could have been related to many different things. I just knew it was a significant change.

Q. And you felt it was a significant change that a doctor should know about?

A. Yes.

Q. Did you call – or you tried to call a doctor at that time, didn't you?

A. I did place a call to Dr. Moores, yes.

Q. And was it in your first observation of him on the 25th that you felt the doctor should be called?

A. Yes.

Q. And it looked to me like that was at eight o'clock when you first assessed Mr. Gonzales on the morning of the 25th; is that right? You might look at page 183. Well, first look at 183.

A. I documented my assessment at 8:00 a.m. The assessment would have been completed prior to that time.

Q. The physical assessment; the actual doing the assessment?

A. Yes.

Q. Do you recall how much sooner you would have done the physical assessment or what's typical?

A. Most likely, 10 to 15 minutes prior.

Q. Do you remember any conversations you had with Mrs. Gonzales at that time?

A. Not specifically. I did talk to her. I can remember she was concerned. I cannot recall what was said.

Q. She was concerned about his altered mental status.

A. Yes.

Q. I found an entry made at page 201 by a Miss Holter, a student nurse. Do you find that?

A. Yes.

Q. Now, she is a student, but apparently she was authorized to provide care to Mr. Gonzales at that time. Do you remember Miss Holter?

A. No.

Q. And that entry was at 7:20. Do you recall or would you have directed her to do that or would that just be a function she knew to do on her own?

A. She would have done that on her own.

Q. She noted, too, that the gentleman was at least confused and drowsy and hard to awaken.

A. Yes.

Q. And that would suggest, would it not, some type of altered mental status?

A. Sometimes.

Q. What else could it suggest?

A. It could also suggest he was asleep and she woke him up. So he was confused and drowsy.

Q. One page 201, just to the left of that, there was an entry at eight o'clock the night before.

A. Yes.

Q. Do you know whether you would have – and I know you don't see this paper copy when you're in the hospital; is that correct?

A. You don't see the paper copy, but you can pull up the screen on the Care Manager to look at this.

Q. Do you recall whether you did do that based upon your own assessment that was recorded at eight o'clock? Did you go back through and look to see what his status, mental status had been in previous assessments?

A. I don't recall if I looked on the computer.

Q. Would it have been your habit and practice to do so?

A. Sometimes –

Q. Okay.

A. —after receiving report from the off-going nurse.

Q. And your note at eight o'clock on page 201, it says under Neuro Assessment "Normal except."

A. Yes.

Q. Do you know why you chose that?

A. His neurological assessment was not normal.

Q. And that's explained, I guess, in part by the next entry. You said Orientation/LOC.

A. Yes.

Q. You said, "Alert." What does that refer to?

A. He was awake. His eyes were opening spontaneously. I didn't have to arouse him at that time.

Q. Okay, what about stuperous? What does that mean?

A. He was very confused. Stuperous is a term a little bit more than confused. Generally when someone is somewhat drowsy, very confused, unable to make their needs known.

Q. Do you recall what he – what his communication was that caused you to believe that was a more appropriate description?

A. As I recall, he could not answer any questions. He could not follow my commands at that time.

Q. Look at the next page of your notes. It says "the patient unable to keep focus on any person or object."

A. Yes.

Q. What should we picture in terms of the behavior of the patient that probably caused you to make that entry?

A. That when I would ask him a question or direct him to do something, though he might look at me at the time I was speaking as opposed to doing what I had asked, he would look away or just not do what I had asked.

Q. Which probably would cause the questioner or you to wonder, I wonder if he's hearing me. I wonder if he really knows what I'm saying.

A. I wonder if he understands what I'm saying.

Q. Okay. Let's look at page 183. At eight o'clock, this same assessment, you did a neuro check.

A. Yes.

Q. And again, you make the entry alert, stuperous, but under eye opening, it says "3 to speech." What does that mean?

A. It means if anyone is talking to him, he would open his eyes.

Q. Okay. Why is the number 3 there?

A. The neuro check involves a Glasgow coma scale. And it assigns numeric value to patient's responses on this scale and the total numerical value then determines their level of consciousness.

Q. Correct. But what is the range that one could pick from in the fall of 2006 between 3 and some other number?

A. I believe the range for eye opening is 1 to 4.

Q. So –

A. I believe it's 4.

Q. On that scale, 3 would be, of course, obviously less than 4.

A. Yes.

Q. What behavior would you see in a patient that you believe would cause you to characterize it or quantify it as 3 verses 4?

A. That is very objective, if the patient opens their eyes when you talk to them, they get a 3 a opposed to they're awake, looking around, everything is fine, that's a 4.

Q. Let me ask you this. Does it communicate something less than full mental state, normal mental states with respect to the eye opening?

A. It depends on the situation.

Q. In any event, when you added up your numbers, he would have gotten one taken away from 15 at least because of that?

A. Yes.

Q. The next one says Best Verbal Response, and it has number 2, incomplete sounds. Can you describe what that means?

A. It's incomprehensible sounds. When he would attempt to answer me, I couldn't understand what he was saying.

Q. And do you know what the values were for that category?

A. 1 to 5.

Q. Okay. Best motor response, you have a number 5, localized pain. Can you tell me why you made that entry?

A. Best motor response is a test that determines their ability to follow commands. So Mr. Gonzales on the morning of the 25th would not obey my commands to move his extremities, but if I applied pressure, he would move that extremity. That's what localized pain means.

Q. And it looks like you assessed a Glasgow score of 10?

A. Yes.

Q. What is done, then, with Glasgow scores?

A. It's just a number to help us determine the patient's level of consciousness. There's not like a formula that if their number is this, then you do that. It just helps determine the patient's condition.

Q. Is there written guidelines that – not necessarily even from the hospital, but just written guidelines that give a better description or just give a description of a 10, what that patient probably is having for mental status?

A. I'm not sure.

Q. Then going on to the next page, 237, there's some comments. And the first comment – one of the comments is, "Unable to determine as patient cannot answer questions at this time." That refers to the location of the pain. What behavior in a patient do you think probably caused you to make that entry?

A. I use the FLACC scale to determine his pain. When I asked him where his pain was, he made incomprehensible sounds. He couldn't tell me where it was.

Q. Do you understand he probably tried? He was verbalizing, but couldn't be understood?

A. I couldn't determine if he was answering my questions or if he was just making sounds.

Q. And then also, it says here, the last of those comments, "called Dr. Moores' answering service."

A. Yes.

Q. "Waiting for call back."

A. Yes.

Q. Do you know why you called Dr. Moores?

A. Due to the patient's change in level of consciousness.

Q. He was on the orthopedic floor at the time?

A. The surgical floor.

Q. Do you know, was there an orthopedic surgeon that was taking care of him?

A. Yes.

Q. And who was that?

A. Dr. Ramish

Q. Did you try and call Dr. Ramish?

A. No.

Q. And why not?

A. Because Dr. Moores was the attending physician.

Q. It says, "waiting for call back." You say there you got his answering service. Did you try again to call Dr. Moores or do you know what became of that call that you placed?

A. Dr. Moores returned my call.

Q. He did return your call?

A. Yes.

Q. Do you recall that?

A. Yes.

Q. You have a memory of it?

A. Uh-hum.

Q. Is it documented here somewhere?

A. It is – it would be documented.

Q. What page are you on?

A. 259.

Q. All right, go ahead.

A. He returned my call at 8:46.

Q. Six, it appears. 8:46?

A. Yes. AM.

Q. And do you have an independent recollection of the conversation?

A. No.

Q. Okay. But you know you did because it's in the notes here?

A. Right.

Q. Okay. And tell me what he said, then, based on your note. What did he say?

A. In my review of the chart, he ordered lab work.

Q. Do you know what he ordered or do we know? Can we see in the record what he ordered?

A. It's in the record in one of the doctor's orders.

Q. Okay. Sure. Do you find that on page 54?

A. Yes.

Q. And then read it. I believe it says, "Stat ABG, please."

A. Yes.

Q. "TO" which might mean telephone order?

A. Yes.

Q. "Dr. Moores," and then it's got a slash and somebody RN. Do you know who that is?

A. That is Joanne Norris.

Q. How do you spell her name, do you know?

A. I don't want to spell it wrong.

Q. Don't worry about it, it's not important. The time is 8:55, correct?

A. For that order?

Q. Yes, uh-huh.

(Break.)

Q. Why don't you read the whole thing, time and everything?

A. On 9/25/06 at 8:50, "digoxin level, CBC with diff. Ammonia level and CMP were ordered now." Read back and verified from Dr. Moores to myself, Eric Snow, RN.

Q. Can we imagine then, you were probably still on the orthopedic or surgical floor when you got this callback?

A. Yes.

Q. And he directly gave you that instruction?

A. Over the phone.

Q. Would you have written it down on a pad of paper as you were speaking?

A. It would depend.

Q. Okay. Did you immediately, do you think, make this entry in the paper record, then?

A. Yes.

Q. If you know, what is the significance of the word "now" to you? When it says do some things and it says now.

A. That signifies to me and to the lab that they have a short amount of time to get the results back. The lab work has to be drawn within half an hour.

Q. Okay. And then the next entry, then, is at 8:55. It appears – at least the numbers are 8:55 by Nurse Norris. And you noted that at what time?

A. 9:10 a.m.

Q. Do you have an independent recall of any of this? I mean the conversation, trying to get a hold of Dr. Moores and the conversation back, your noting of those things?

A. Not really.

Q. Okay. How were those – accomplished, the orders that he gave you?

A. When we receive orders, they're put into the computer electronically, which is then transmitted to the department that needs to know, and the lab would have come up, sent a phlebotomist up to obtain the blood work and the cardiopulmonary department would have sent somebody to get arterial blood gases.

Q. Thank you, Nurse Snow; I have no further questions.

Chapter 25
Case Study: Mr. X

Rosale Lobo, RN MSN, CNS, LNCC
CONFIDENTIAL WORK PRODUCT
TO: Law Firm
RE: Mr. X

Mr. X was admitted to Y Hospital on January 11, 2007, for arthroscopic bilateral knee replacements. On the admission papers there was documentation that stated he had reddened raised areas below the knee, lower back and feet. It was noted that he had a pressure ulcer, but it could not be staged. His labs showed that he was anemic: Hgb 11.3 (13.5 – 18) and his Hct 34.1 (40-54). These values were consistently low during this first hospitalization. The notes also stated that his skin was moist and he had eczema.

On January 12, 2007, post-operatively; Mr. X required assistance to turn in the bed. He was wearing pressure boots to the bottom of his legs, as they are used to prevent blood clots from knee surgery. Physical therapy made notes that he required 2-3 people to get him from the bed to the chair. His skin integrity was further compromised because he developed "foot drop". There is even an entry by nutrition that Mr. X's skin had an unstageable decubitus to his lower back.

There are numerous nursing entries alluding to Mr. X's very moist skin and his diaphoresis.

By January 15, 2007, nurses described Mr. X's skin as having stage 2 partial thickness skin loss. The skin is documented as being blistered and broken, measuring 2 cm x 4 cm on both sides, draining sanguineous fluid. At this time, he was seen by a wound care nurse.

Y Hospital's physical therapy and medical team determined that he was not meeting his PT goals and they decided to transfer him to Z Facility for intensive rehabilitation.

The intra-agency transfer form (W-10) was completed and does not have any information to alert Z Facility that there was a wound care diagnosis and treatment.

When Mr. X was evaluated at Z Facility on January 15, 2007, they deemed that he had an unstageable wound to both sides of his buttocks and gluteal crease. There was a suggestion that he be placed on a Plexus mattress, but there is no documentation that this was done.

The following day, someone documented that the decubitus is a stage 4 with inflamed surrounding tissue and there was swelling to the inner thigh. On January 19, 2007, a nurse documented that the wound was draining serosanginous fluid.

On January 20, 2007, Mr. X had a temperature of 100.3. This prompted a visit from the medical doctor on January 21, 2007. The physician ordered a wound care nurse to evaluate and treat. The following day, Mr. X was taken to Hospital S for a debridement.

Summary:

Mr. X's skin was at a high risk for skin breakdown because he entered the hospital with a reddened area, he has eczema and produced a lot of sweat. He became a higher risk after surgery when he developed the bilateral foot drop, making it very difficult to get out of bed and move around. There was inconsistent skin care that started at Y Hospital and continued while he was a patient at Z Facility.

Please Note:

This summary is written from the plaintiff's point of view. There are several areas where the nurse could have documented to prove that the standard of care was being met or where the patient might have been non-adherent to the plan of care. Create entries that support your attempts to follow the plan, because charting by exception leaves too much to the imagination.

What information would help the nurses demonstrate that the standard of care had been met?

Perhaps the skin care log, or the turning and repositioning schedule, and as important, Mr. X's response to the interventions. Completing the paperwork so the interventions match the orders. When there is an unfortunate outcome, the paper trail becomes the strongest piece of evidence.

Chapter 26
Case Study: Nursing Home

Rosale Lobo, RN, Legal Nurse Consultant
CONFIDENTIAL MEMORANDUM
TO: Law Firm
RE: Significant Events

Dear Attorney,

I have reviewed the medical record and these are the entries that tell the story from the client's perspective.

70 y/o male, 5'8, 200 lbs., brought to Nursing Home by his wife and son 5 days post-operative for a right shunt occlusion craniectomy. He was brought directly to the LTC facility after he was discharged from the hospital. It is not clear why the hospital did not provide transportation. He was admitted at 8 p.m. and discharged at 7 a.m. the following morning.

The patient's wife provided the following information:
- He has been incontinent of urine since the surgery.
- He has an unsteady gait and will attempt to ambulate without assistance.
- He has short-term memory loss and is confused in new situations since the surgery.

Information obtained from the nursing documentation:
- Wandering, Anxious, Short-Term Memory Problem (no recall after 5 min.).
- Modified independence – difficult in new situations.
- Wears glasses.
- Bladder – Briefs/Pads - has chronic urinary incontinence.
- Wheelchair as the primary mode of transportation, but he can ambulate independently.
- Assisted to the bathroom x 2 during the evening.

Vital Signs:
8 p.m. - 99.2, 66,18, 144/64 (Admission)
11 p.m. – 7 a.m. – 98.1, 58, 20, 130/78 (Shift assessment)
5 a.m. – 98.1, 58, 20, 130/76
6 a.m. – 120/70 (Lying down) and 130/87 (sitting)
7 a.m. – 126/80, 20, 58 (before being transferred to a hospital for further evaluation)

Mental Status:
Short–term memory loss
Anxious in new situations
Wandering behavior

Summary:
During the client's brief stay at a LTC, he was apparently assisted to the bathroom twice during the early morning. At 6 a.m., he was found on the floor, face down.

Issues to consider:
- Why did they take his blood pressure at 5 a.m. and 6 a.m.? Orders were for once every shift for the first 24 hours, a positional blood pressure once per week.
- Why would someone walk him to the bathroom at 4 a.m. and 5 a.m.?
- Notes stated that he was ambulated to the bathroom.
- He was supposed to be mobilized in a wheelchair.
- He was unable to control his bladder and was wearing pads. He didn't need to go to the bathroom to void.
- What standards of care would be used to identify if a patient was being managed accordingly?

If the patient was documented as having an unsteady gait and was a fall risk, did the nurses have an obligation to place him in a safe situation? For example, should he have been placed near the nursing station so that he could be watched? Should the nurse have placed him in a wheelchair and moved him around or perhaps the nurse should have placed him in a recliner? What about calling the family and having them come back and watch the patient? Should the nurse have called the physician to request advice?

If you were the nurse caring for this patient, what interventions would you have put into place to maintain safety? How would you defend the care provided?

Please note - The Veteran's Administration (VA) hospital does not allow the family to be responsible for the patient's safety while they are hospitalized. They use sitters or "continuous safety monitors."

Chapter 27
Deposition of Chase Patrick, RN
Taken by the Plaintiff

Appearances

For the Plaintiff:	*Attorney: Jorge Claire*
For the Defendant: *Chase Patrick*	*Attorney: Ivy Young*
For the Defendant: *Nursing Home*	*Attorney: Darlene Friedland*

(This is an excerpt of the deposition already in progress)

Q. My question in general: When you were at Nursing Home in 2008, were there circumstances upon which you, in fact, utilized a geri-chair in reference to a patient who was in danger of injuring himself by falling out of bed?

A. Yes. I would say that patient—if the patient got fall—fell before or had a tendency to constantly get out of bed, that's when I would use it.

Q. All right. And at Nursing Home in 2008, all right?

A. Uh-huh.

Q. That's the time—

A. Yeah.

Q. —that this accident happened.

A. That's the time.

Q. They had geri-chairs at Nursing Home. Correct?

A. Yes.

Q. And the geri-chairs at Nursing Home at that time could be moved around. Correct?

A. Yes.

Q. So you could take a patient in 2008 such at Mr. Patient or another patient, you could help them into a geri-chair, and you could move the geri-chair down to the nursing station.

A. Yes. I would do that.

Q. All right. And the reason you would do that is because they could be observed and have—they could be observed at the nursing station, correct?

A. Yeah. Because—and also, even if they are at the nursing station, that cannot prevent them from falling.

Q. All right, now in addition, when you take a patient in a geri-chair —this is in 2008 at Nursing Home—down to the nursing station, the patient also has contact with a nurse at the nursing station. Correct?

A. But at the nursing station, you know, it depends on the time, because sometimes the CNA is busy, the nurse is busy, you are in the ward watching the patient. And also, sometimes it's not like you—is one and one with the patient because you have other patients to do.

Q. Well, let me ask you this: In June, all right —

A. Uh-huh.

Q. —when this happened in June of 2008, was the nursing station at Nursing Home where Mr. Patient was in his area, was that manned at all times? Was there a person there at all times in the nursing station?

A. Yeah. There's time you have to move. If another patient is calling, you have to go to answer it—to answer it, to answer the call light, you know?

Q. So are you saying to me that at Nursing Home in June 2008, that there were times when there was no nurse or no personnel in the nursing station?

A. There are nurses at the nursing station. But on the unit you don't stay at the nurses' station all the time. You go in to the patients' rooms, too.

Q. All right. I just want to make sure my question is clear.

A. Uh-huh.

Q. I'm not talking about an individual nurse—

A. Uh-huh.

Q. —who has got—or a CNA or LPN who has got duties.

A. Uh-huh.

Q. I'm talking about in June of 2008—

A. Uh-huh.

Q. —was it the—was there always a person, whether an RN or LPN, at the nursing station on the eleven to seven shift?

A. Of course, yes.

Q. At all times?

A. All times.

Q. All right.

A. Yeah, two nurses.

STOP

BEGIN

Q. So you knew, when you came in at approximately 12:15, 12:30 —all right—that this man was incontinent of urine. Correct?

A. Yes.

Q. Which means he had no control over his bladder. Correct?

A. Yes.

Q. And you knew that potentially, somebody who is incontinent of urine would attempt to go — get up and go to the bathroom. Correct?

A. Yes.

Q. And you knew that at 12:30. Correct?

A. Uh-huh.

Q. And that you also knew that in reference to his bowel status, which means when he would have a bowel movement, when he would want to go to the bathroom, that was uncertain. Correct?

A. Yes.

Q. And you knew by reading this note at approximately 12:15 or 12:30, that this patient attempts to get out of bed without —out of bed frequently without assistance, you knew that?

A. Yes.

Q. And you also knew that he had an unsteady gait. Correct?

A. Yes.

Q. Because in addition to the verbal tape, you were required— in fact, you did read this note.

A. Uh-huh.

Q. Correct?

A. Yes.

Q. So you knew that this gentleman—you knew his age. Correct?

A. Yes.

Q. How old was he?

A. I don't know. I don't remember.

Q. Well, why don't you look at the chart?

A. Seventy-four.

Q. All right. So here's what you knew at 12:30. Correct?

A. Uh-huh.

Q. Based on this note, you knew that he was 73, 74 years old. Correct?

A. Yes.

Q. You knew that he was post-operation, very serous operation. Correct?

A. Yes.

Q. You knew he had a hole in his head. Correct?

A. Yes.

Q. You knew that he had a shunt. Correct?

A. Uh-huh. Yes.

Q. You knew that he was incontinent of urine. Correct?

A. Yes.

Q. Which means you knew that he had pads. Correct?

A. Yes.

Q. And you knew that he would attempt to get up and leave the bed frequently without assistance. Correct?

A. Yes.

Q. And you knew at that time that he had an unsteady gait. Correct?

A. Yes.

Q. And you knew, based on these facts, that this man was a fall risk. Correct?

A. Yes.

Q. So you knew it was your responsibility to make sure that this man didn't fall. Isn't that correct?

A. Yes.

Q. And you were Mr. Patient's nurse. Correct?

A. Yes.

Q. There was no other nurse that had responsibility for Mr. Patient; you had that nursing responsibility. Correct?

A. Yes.

Q. And you had the nursing responsibility to, in fact, supervise the CNA. Correct?

A. Yes.

Q. And you had the responsibility to make sure that, in addition to yourself, that the CNA protected Mr. Patient. Correct?

A. Yes.

Q. And you had the responsibility to tell the CNA that Mr. Patient was incontinent of urine. Correct?

A. Yes.

Q. And you had the responsibility to tell the CNA that this patient attempts to get up and leave the bed frequently without assistance. Correct?

A. Yes.

Q. And you had the responsibility to inform the CNA that this man had an unsteady gait. Correct?

A. Yes.

Q. All right. Now did the CNA have a responsibility at this time on June 18, 19 – reviewing this chart, did she have a responsibility to read these notes, also?

A. I usually tell the CNA verbally. Some of them will look at the chart also to know more about the patient.

Q. So are you telling me it's also the responsibility of the CNA to read the nurses' notes?

A. If they want to. It's not—you usually tell them what they need to do for the patient.

Q. So it's not — So you are saying it's not the responsibility of the CNA to read these notes. It's your responsibility to read them and tell the CNA. Is that correct?

A. Yeah, They can read it, also. They can read it.

Q. All right. Now, looking at this chart, when do you usually —when is your practice and procedure to make notes on a patient?

A. Usually, at the end of my shift, I usually do the notes.

Q. All right. So you don't make any notes on an interim basis?

A. Unless there's really an emergency; a patient got a new order, I call the doctor. I usually do it right away in case something that night is going on. If it's nothing really emergency, or everything seems okay, I usually leave it until the end of my shift.

Q. All right. Now, when you make your notes at the end of the— do you make any interim notes? In other words, do you make notes on a separate piece of paper or a pad on an interim basis?

A. Yes.

Q. All right. In other words, and then you transfer those to the chart?

A. Yes.

Q. And on what document do you do that?

A. They have a patient roster sheet. When I'm taking the report or while I was listening to the tale, I will designate for the patient the room number. I will write their names, take the report. Whenever I did something for them, I will put the time and what I did for them.

Q. All right. Now—but you don't do that all the time?

A. All the time. All the time.

Q. All the time?

A. Yeah.

Q. So you are telling me, in this case, that you have another piece of paper that has notes on it as to what you did—

A. Yes.

Q. —for this patient between 12:30—

A. Yes.

Q. —and seven o' clock?

A. Yes.

Q. Where is that piece of paper?

A. So I usually keep it for two or three days and then throw it in the trash.

Q. Well, you knew in this case that Mr. Patient fell out of bed. Correct?

A. Yes.

Q. And you knew that Mr. Patient was injured. Correct?

A. Yes.

Q. And you knew you had to fill out an incident report. Correct?

A. Yes.

Q. And you did fill out an incident report. Correct?

A. Yes.

Q. And are you telling me that knowing that you had an incident report that you had to do and this patient was injured, you threw the piece of paper away that you made notes on?

A. Yeah. I usually don't keep my papers. Usually, after two or three days, I finish with them because I didn't know the patient was injured severely or died or whatever. When you finish, you usually put it in—you just leave it. I don't keep them. If I have to keep every paper, how many papers will I have? Because I don't know what's going to happen. I never know they will have a suit pending. I didn't know. I don't keep my paper, the note, my writing on the little report I take. I don't keep it.

Q. Well, you don't keep it in the usual event. And are you telling me when a patient is injured, you don't keep your handwritten notes?

A. No. No.

Q. All right. Are you telling me that you transcribed all your written notes that you had on that piece of paper to this sheet?

A. Yes.

Q. Is that what you are telling me?

A. Yes. Yes. Yes.

Q. You transcribed everything?

A. Yes. Anytime I have to do something for the patient, even to give them medicine or whatever, I put the time. If they request something, I put it on my little report paper before I transcribe it to the chart.

STOP

BEGIN

Q. All right. So even though you instructed him how to use the call bell—right? — that —and the call bell was in reach, you had no assurance, in reference to Mr. Patient, that he would use the call bell. Isn't that true?

A. But when you talk to the patient, he seems to understand. So —

Q. Well, I'm saying to you, you knew about the patient —

A. Uh-huh.

Q. —it's in the chart, that he would forget things within five minutes. Right? And you knew he was confused and forgetful. That's in your own note. Correct?

A. Yes.

Q. So you knew even if you told him to use the call bell to alert you to get up, that he would potentially forget about that in five minutes. Correct?

A. Yes.

Q. And so when you were there, you had no assurance that he would use the call bell. Isn't that true?

A. I don't know.

Q. Well, wait a minute. You knew that—

A. I know. But sometimes the patient forgets, but might not use it. You never know.

Q. Excuse me. You knew at that time—you knew at that time that because of his condition of being forgetful, not remembering stuff five minutes later—things five minutes later and being confused, that you as a nurse could not rely on him to warn you that he was getting out of bed or had a problem by pushing a call button. Isn't that true?

A. That's true. That's one of the reasons, yes. He had the bed alarm, too, to alert us when he tried to get out of bed.

Q. All right. And as a matter of fact, because you knew that he was in danger of those circumstances—right? —that a call button was going to help you, you called the supervisor, made the supervisor aware and asked for a bed alarm to be applied for safety. Isn't that true?

A. Yes.

Q. And the reason that you called for the bed alarm and asked the supervisor to give you a bed alarm is because you, at the time, made a decision that this man could get out of bed without any notice and injure himself. Isn't that true?

A. Yes.

Q. All right. And so you called the supervisor. Correct?

A. Yes.

Q. And right at that time, at four o'clock in the morning, he did not have a bed alarm. Correct?

A. I don't remember. I don't remember if he had one. I don't know. So I requested it from the supervisor.

Q. Well, your notes says—okay? —your note says, first of all, you said he's toileted and ambulated with assistance and voided a normal amount. Correct?

A. Yes.

Q. So that means you took him out of bed, put him in a wheelchair and then took him to the bathroom. Correct?

A. Yes.

Q. And you also observed that his gait was unsteady. Correct?

A. Yes.

Q. So after you observed—you took him to the bathroom— right? —and you observed his gait was unsteady. And with all the other factors, you then called the supervisor and said you wanted to have a bed alarm applied to this patient. Correct?

A. Yes.

Q. And you wanted to do it for safety. Correct?

A. Yes.

Q. Now, a bed alarm is not going to keep him in the bed. Correct?

A. No. That won't keep him in the bed but—

Q. The only thing a bed alarm is going to do it tell you that Mr. Patient is out of bed?

A. He's trying—He's trying to get out of bed.

Q. Either trying to get out of bed or is out of the bed. Correct?

A. Yes.

Q. And once the alarm goes off, the alarm stays on until a nurse or CNA turns it off?

A. Yes. We'll go see what's going on with the patient.

Q. Now, did you need any paperwork to get the bed alarm from the supervisor?

A. No.

Q. Who brings it up? She brings it up personally?

A. Yes.

Q. So you don't even have a bed alarm on the floor. You have to ask the supervisor for a bed alarm?

A. You can have it on the floor. But by the time you look for it, the supervisor will bring you one they got in hand or in the office.

Q. So it's quicker to have the supervisor—

A. Yes. By the time you check, you know—

Q. Right.

A. —you have it.

Q. So that means you can stay with the patient?

A. Yes.

Q. Right?

A. Or the CNA stay—

Q. You can stay with the patient until the bed alarm comes. Right?

A. Yes.

Q. And that's what you did here. Correct?

A. Yes.

Q. In other words, you didn't leave this patient once you determined that the patient was unsteady, gait was unsteady—right? —you knew he was confused and forgetful, you stayed right with him until the supervisor brought you the bed alarm. Right?

A. And the reason you did that was because you were concerned that the patient might get out of bed again and fall. Correct?

Q. Yes.

STOP

Part 4:
The Helpful
Resources Side
Appendices

Appendix A
Common Legal Terms

Acknowledgement – The signature of a clerk or attorney certifying that the person filing the document has sworn that the contents are true, and/or that the document is signed by his or her free act and deed.

Action – Also called a case or lawsuit. A civil judicial proceeding where one party sues another for a wrong done, or to protect a right or to prevent a wrong.

Adjournment – Postponement of a court session until another time or place.

Affirmation – Declaring something to be true under the penalty of perjury by a person who will not take an oath for religious or other reasons.

Affidavit – A written statement made under oath.

Allegation – Saying that something is true. The assertion, declaration or statement of a party in a case, made in a pleading.

Answer – A court document, or pleading, in a civil case, by which the defendant responds to the plaintiff's complaint.

Appeal – Asking a higher court to review the decision or sentence of a trial court because the lower court made an error.

Appearance – The official court form filed with the court clerk which tells the court that you are representing yourself in a lawsuit or criminal case or that an attorney is representing you. All court notices and calendars will be mailed to the address listed on the forms. When a defendant in a civil case files an appearance, the person the person is submitting to the court's jurisdiction.

Appellant – The party appealing a decision or judgment to a higher court.

Appellee – The party against whom an appeal is taken.

Arbitration – Submitting a case or dispute to designated parties for a decision, instead of using a judge.

Arraignment – The first court appearance of a person accused of a crime. The person is advised of his or her rights by a judge and may respond to the criminal charges by entering a plea. Usually, this happens the morning after a person is arrested.

Attachment – A lien on property or assets to hold it to pay or satisfy any final judgment.

Attorney of Record – Attorney whose name appears in the permanent records or files of a case.

Bar – Refers to attorneys as a group.

Brief – A written document prepared by a lawyer or party on each side of a dispute and filed with the court in support of their arguments.

Calendar – A list of court cases scheduled for specific dates and times.

Capias Mittimus – A civil arrest warrant used to get a person physically into court to respond to a specific case or claim.

Case – A lawsuit or action in a court.

Case Conference – A meeting scheduled by the court to review the case.

Case File – The court file containing papers submitted in a case.

Certify – To testify in writing; to make known or establish as a fact.

Charge – Formal accusation of a crime.

Charge to Jury – In a trial practice, an address delivered by the court to the jury at the close of the case instructing the jury as to what principles of law they are to apply in reaching a decision.

Complaint – A legal document that tells the court what you want, which is served with a summons on the defendant to begin the case.

Contempt of Court – A finding that someone disobeyed a court order. Can also mean disrupting court, for ex-ample, being loud or disrespectful in court.

Continuance Date – Date on which the case will next be heard in court.

Costs – Expenses in prosecuting or defending a case in court; usually does not include attorney's fees.

Count – The different parts of a complaint, which could each be a basis or grounds of the lawsuit.

Court Clerk – The person who maintains the official court records of a case. The court clerks' office receives all court papers and assigns hearing dates.

Court Monitor – The person who prepares a written record of the court hearing for a fee, if requested, from audiotapes made during the hearing.

Court Reporter – The person who records everything said during the court hearing on a stenograph machine, and prepares a written record for a fee, if requested.

Court Trial – Trial by a judge, rather than a jury.

Cross-Examination – Questioning by a party or the attorney of an adverse party or a witness.

Damages – Money a party receives as compensation for a legal wrong.

Default – To fail to respond or answer to the plaintiff's claims by filing the required court document; usually an Appearance or an Answer.

Defendant – In civil cases, the person who is given court papers; also called the respondent.

Deposition – Testimony of a witness, taken under oath in response to another party's questions. Testimony is given outside the courtroom, usually in a lawyer's office. A word-for-word account (transcript) is made of the testimony.

Discovery – A formal request by one party in a lawsuit to have information or facts known by the other parties or witnesses disclosed.

Dismissal – A judge's decision to end the case.

Dispose – Ending a legal case or a judicial proceeding.

Disposition – The manner in which a case is settled or resolved.

Docket Number – A unique number the court clerk assigned to a case. It must be used on all future papers filed in the court case.

Evidence – Testimony, documents or objects presented at trial to prove a fact.

Failure to Appear – In a civil case, failing to file an Appearance form.

Felony – Any criminal offense for which a person may be sentenced to a term of imprisonment of more than one year.

Filing – Giving the court clerk legal papers which become part of the case file.

Financial Affidavit – A sworn statement of income, expenses, property (called assets) and debts (called liabilities).

Finding – The court's or jury's decision on issues of fact.

Garnishment – A court order to collect money or property.
Grievance – A complaint filed against an attorney or judge, claiming an injury or injustice.

Hearsay – Testimony given by a witness who tells second- or third-hand information.

Hung Jury – A jury whose members cannot reconcile their differences of opinion and thus cannot reach a verdict.

Injunction – A court order to stop doing or to start doing a specific act.

Interrogatory – Formal, written questions used to get information from another party in a lawsuit.

Judge – A person who hears and decides cases for the court. Appointed by the governor for a term of eight years and confirmed by the General Assembly.

Judgment – A court decision. Also called a decree or an order.

Judgment File – A permanent court record of the court's final disposition of the case.

Juris Number – An identification number assigned to each attorney in a case.

Jurisdiction – Power and authority of a court to hear and make a judgment in a case.

Juror – Member of a jury.

Jury Charge – The judge's formal instructions on the law to the jury before it begins deliberations.

Jury Instructions – Directions given by the judge to the jury concerning the law of the case.

Lien – A charge, hold or claim upon property of another as security for a debt.

Lis Pendens – A pending lawsuit.

Litigant – A party to the case.

Mediation – A dispute resolution process in which an impartial third party assists the parties to voluntarily reach a mutually acceptable settlement.

Mitigating Circumstances – Circumstances that may be considered to reduce the guilt of a defendant. Usually based on fairness or mercy.

Modification – Request to change a prior order. Usually required showing a change in circumstances since the date of the prior order.

Motion – Usually written request to the court.

Movant – The person who filed the motion, or request to the court.

Moving Party – The person making the request to the court in a case.

Ne Exeat – A legal paper requesting that a person be required to remain within the jurisdiction of the court (either through incarceration or posting of a bond).

No Contest – A plea in a criminal case that allows the defendant to be convicted without admitting guilt for the crime charged.

Non-Suit – Vacating a case by the court, usually for failure to prosecute.

Notarize – To formally complete a document by acknowledgement or oath.

Oath – To swear/affirm to the truth of a statement/document.

Order – A written direction of a court or judge to do or refrain from doing certain acts.

Parties – The people or legal entities who are named as plaintiff(s) and defendants(s) on legal papers.

Perjury – Making false statements under oath.

Petition – A formal written request to a court, which starts a special proceeding.

Petitioner – Another word for plaintiff; the person starting the lawsuit.

Plaintiff – The person who sues or starts a civil case, also called the petitioner or the complainant.

Pleadings – The court documents filed with the court by the parties in a civil case.

Post Judgment – Any request to a court or action by a judge after a judgment in a case.

Pretrial – A conference with a judge or trial referee to discuss discovery and settlement.

Pretrial Hearing – Conference with attorneys to determine the scope of possible trial, with a view towards resolving issues through agreement.

Promise to Appear – A type of non-financial bond where the defendant agrees to return to court without giving cash or property.

Pro Se – A Latin phrase meaning for "yourself" – representing oneself in any kind of case.

Ready – Means ready to start the trial or begin oral arguments. Usually said by an attorney or party in response to a judge calling the list of a scheduled case.

Record – The pleadings, the exhibits and the transcript made by the court reporter of all proceedings in a trial.

Respondent – Another word for defendant, the person responding to a lawsuit.

Rest – To be done presenting the evidence in a case, as in "the plaintiff rests."

Restitution – Money ordered to be paid by the defendant to the victim to reimburse the victim for the cost of the crime. Generally making good or giving the equivalent for any loss, damages, or injury caused by a person's actions.

Rule to Show Cause – Summons compelling a person to appear in court on a specific date.

Service – The legal method for giving a copy of the court papers being filed to other parties in a case.

Short Calendar – A list of cases in which hearings by the judge or magistrate is requested or required.

Statute – A law enacted by a legislative body.

Statute of Limitations – A certain time allowed by law for starting a case.

Stay – Temporary stopping of a judicial proceeding.

Stipulation – Also called a "stip". A written agreement by the parties or their attorneys.

Subpoena – A command to appear in court to testify as a witness.

Subpoena Duces Tecum – A legal paper requiring someone to produce documents or records for a trial.

Summons – A legal paper that is used to start a civil case and get jurisdiction over a party.

Testimony – Statement made by a witness or party under oath.

Tort – A civil injury or wrong to someone else, or their property.

Transcript – The official written record of everything that was said at a court proceeding, a hearing, or deposition.

Transfer – Assignment of a case to another court location by court order.

Vacate – To cancel or rescind a court order.

Venue – A court location.

Voir Dire – "To speak the truth." The process of questioning prospective jurors or witnesses about their qualifications.

Witness – A person who testifies as to what they saw, heard, observed or did.

Writ – Legal papers filed to start various types of civil lawsuits.

Appendix B
Important Definitions and Standard of Practice Statements

National Council of State Boards of Nursing

The practice of nursing is regulated by state boards of nursing in each state. In each state, the model nurse practice act describes the scope of practice for registered nursing, licensed practical/vocational nurses, and advanced practice nurses. A model nurse practice act has been developed by NCSBN to serve as a guide for boards of nursing.

License is the process by which boards of nursing grant permission to an individual to engage in nursing practice after determining that the applicant has attained the competency necessary to perform a unique scope of practice. Licensure is necessary when the regulated activities are complex, require specialized knowledge and skill and independent decision-making. The licensure process determines if the applicant has the necessary skills to safely perform a specified scope of practice by predetermining the criteria needed and to evaluate licensure applicants to determine if they meet criteria. Licensure provides that:

- A specified scope of practice may only be performed legally by licensed individuals.
- Title protection
- Authority to take disciplinary action should the licensee violates the law or rules, in order to ensure that the public is protected.

Certification is another type of credential that affords title protection and recognition of accomplishment, but does not include a legal scope of practice. The federal government has used the term certification to define the credentialing process by which a non-government agency or association recognizes individuals who have met specified requirements. Many state boards of nursing use professional certifications as one requirement towards granting authority for practice to advanced practice registered nurses. Some state government agencies have also used the term certification for government credentialing. Confusion may occur because regulatory agencies and professional associations may use the same term in different contexts.

Medical Record (and purpose)

The purpose of the medical record is to provide a vehicle for: documenting actions taken in patient management; documenting patient progress; providing meaningful medical information to other practitioners should the patient transfer to a new provider or should the provider be unavailable for some reason. A medical record shall include, but not be limited to, information sufficient to justify any diagnosis and treatment rendered, dates of treatment, actions taken by a non-licensed person when ordered or authorized by the provider; doctors' orders, nurses notes and charts, birth certificate work sheets, and any other diagnostic data or documents specified in the rules and regulations. All entries must be signed by the person responsible for them. (Department of Public Health, 19a-14-40.)

Professions Involved

Each person licensed or certified to the following chapters and Acts shall maintain appropriate medical records of the assessment, diagnosis, and course of treatment provided each patient, and such medical records shall be kept for the period prescribed. (Department of Public Health, 19a-14-41.)

(a) Pathology slides, EEG and ECG Tracings must each be kept for seven (7) years. If ECG is taken and the results are unchanged from a previous ECG, then only the most recent results need be retained. Reports on each of these must be kept for the duration of the medical record.

(b) Lab reports and PKU report must be kept for at least five (5) years. Only positive (abnormal) lab results need be retained.

(c) X-Ray films must be kept for three (3) years.

(Department of Public Health, 19a-14-42.)

Exceptions

Nothing in these regulations shall prevent a practitioner from retaining records longer than the prescribed minimum. When medical records for a patient are retained by a healthcare facility or organization, the individual practitioner shall not be required to maintain duplicate records and the retention schedules of the facility or organization shall apply to the records. If a claim of malpractice, unprofessional conduct, or negligence with respect to a particular patient has been made, or litigation has been commenced, then all records for that patient must be retained until the matter is resolved. A consulting healthcare provider need not retain records if they are sent to the referring provider, who must retain them. If a patient requests his records to be transferred to another provider who then becomes the primary provider to the patient, then the first provider is not required to retain that patient's records.

(Department of Public Health, 19a-14-43.)

Example of a Standard written by the Social Security Administration regarding skilled nursing facilities. Section 1891 [42 U.S.C. 1395i-3] (a) Skilled Nursing Facility Defined – In this title, the term "skilled nursing facility" means an institution (or a distinct part of an institution) which –

1. Is primarily engaged in providing to residents
(A) Skilled nursing care and related services for residents who require medical or nursing care, or
(B) Rehabilitation services for the rehabilitation of the injured, disabled, or sick persons and is not primarily for the care and treatment of mental diseases.

A skilled nursing facility must provide 24-hour licensed nursing service which is sufficient to meet nursing needs of its residents and must use the services of a registered professional nurse at least eight consecutive hours a day, seven days a week.

A skilled nursing facility must protect and promote the right of each resident; including the following rights:

Free choice – the right to choose a personal attending physician, to be fully informed in advance about care and treatment, to be fully informed in advance of any changes in care of treatment that may affect the resident's well being, and (except with respect to a resident adjudged incompetent) to participate in planning care and treatment or changes in care and treatment.

Free from restraints – the right to be free from physical or mental abuse, corporal punishment, involuntary seclusion and any physical or chemical restraints imposed for purposes of discipline or convenience and not required to treat the resident's medical symptoms. Restrains may only be imposed:

1. To ensure the physical safety if the resident or other residents
2. Only upon the written order of a physician that specifies the duration and circumstances under which the restraints are to be used (except emergency circumstances specified by the Secretary until such an order could reasonably be obtained).

Resources:

Social Security Online. (2012, April 4). Requirements for, and assuring quality in care, in skilled nursing facilities. Accessed from http://www.ssa.gov/OP_Home/ssact/title18/1819.htm

Appendix C
Discipline Terminology

Accusation – An accusation is a legal document formally charging a registered nurse with a violation(s) of the Nurse Practice Act, and notifying the public that a disciplinary action is pending against that nurse.

Convicted of a crime substantially related to the qualifications, functions and duties of a RN – Can apply to such crimes as embezzlement, child abuse, spousal abuse, battery, theft from a patient or client, or failure to report abuse.

Default Decision – A decision based on the RNs failure to provide a notice of defense after the accusation has been served, or failure to be present at an Administrative Hearing. All charges are deemed true, and the default decision normally results in a revocation of the RN's license.

Effective (Date) – Indicates the date the disciplinary action goes into operation.

Gross Negligence – An extreme departure from the standard of practice for RNs. An extreme departure means the repeated failure to provide the required nursing care or failure to provide care or exercise precaution in a single situation which the nurse knew or should have known, could result in patient harm.

Incompetence – Lack of knowledge or skill in discharging professional obligations as an RN.

Interim Suspension Order – A license is suspended by an Administrative Law Judge due to the seriousness of the allegations in advance of the filing of an accusation and pending a final determination of the licensee's fitness to practice and provide nursing care.

License Denied – The Board denied an initial license application.

Order to Issue Conditional License – The Board grants an initial application. Once licensed, the applicant is placed on probation, and must be monitored by the Board for a set period of time.

Probation – Allows the licensee to practice as an RN under certain restrictions for a set period of time.

Public Reprimand – The Board issues a letter of reprimand for a minor violation against the Nurse Practice Act, with no restrictions on the license.

Revocation Stayed, Probation – RN license is revoked, temporarily and the RN is allowed to practice as a RN under restricted conditions. While on probation, the nurse is monitored.

Revoked/Surrendered License – The Board has revoked the license and the licensee no longer has the right to practice as an RN or to use this title.

Statement of Issue – A legal document, formally charging an applicant for initial licensure, with a violation(s) of the Nursing Practice Act, and notifying the public that a disciplinary action is pending against the applicant.

Stipulated Agreement – A licensee facing disciplinary action by the Board may negotiate a settlement or "stipulated agreement". The stipulation agreement is similar to an out-of-court settlement in civil suits. The Board must vote to approve stipulation agreements.

Supplemental/Amended Accusation Filed – Additional information or amendments have been made to a previously filed accusation.

Suspension – The Board has ordered the licensee not to practice as a registered nurse for a set or indefinite period of time. Suspension may be imposed in disciplinary actions, prior to a probation term, or may be imposed as a result of a violation of probation.

Voluntary Surrender – The licensee has surrender the license as a resolution to a disciplinary matter. The individual can no longer practice nursing in the state.

Writ – A licensee files an appeal in Superior Court asking the court to overturn the Boards disciplinary decision.

Resource:

California Board of Nursing (n.d.). Disciplinary actions and reinstatements. Accessed April 10, 2012 from http://www.rn.ca. gov/enforcement/dispaction.shtml

Appendix D
Individual Boards of Nursing

Alabama: http://www.abn.state.al.us/
Alaska: http://www.dced.state.ak.us/occ/pnur.htm
Arizona: http://www.azboardofnursing.org/
Arkansas: http://www.state.ar.us/nurse
California RN: http://www.rn.ca.gov/
California VN: http://www.bvnpt.ca.gov/
Colorado: http://www.dora.state.co.us/nursing/
Connecticut: http://www.state.ct.us/dph/
Florida: http://www.doh.state.fl.us/mqa/nursing/rnhome.htm
Georgia PN: http://www.sos.state.ga.us/ebd-lpn/
Georgia RN: http://www.sos.state.ga.us/ebd-rn/
Hawaii: http://www.state.hi.us/dcca/pvloffline/
Idaho: http://www.state.id.us/ibn/ibnhome.htm
Illinois: http://www.dpr.state.il.us/
Indiana: http://www.state.in.us/hbp/isbn/
Iowa: http://www.state.ia.us/government/nursing/
Kansas: http://www.ksbn.org
Kentucky: http://www.kbn.state.ky.us/
Louisiana PN: http://www.lsbpne.com/
Louisiana RN: http://www.lsbn.state.la.us/
Maine: http://www.state.me.us/nursingbd/
Maryland: http://dhmh1d.dhmh.state.md.us/mbn/
Massachusetts: http://www.state.ma.us/reg/boards/rn/
Michigan: http://www.cis.state.mi.us/bhser/genover.htm
Minnesota: http://www.nursingboard.state.mn.us/
Mississippi: http://www.msbn.state.ms.us/webtest
Missouri: http://www.ecodev.state.mo.us/pr/nursing/
Montana: http://www.com.state.mt.us/License/POL/index.htm
Nebraska: http://www.hhs.state.ne.us/crl/nns.htm
Nevada: http://www.nursingboard.state.nv.us
New Hampshire: http://www.state.nh.us/nursing/
New Jersey: http://www.state.nj.us/lps/ca/medical.htm
New Mexico: http://www.state.nm.us/clients/nursing
New York: http://www.nysed.gov/prof/nurse.htm

North Carolina: http://www.ncbon.com/
North Dakota: http://www.ndbon.org/
Ohio: http://www.state.oh.us/nur/
Oregon: http://www.osbn.state.or.us/
Pennsylvania: http://www.dos.state.pa.us/bpoa/nurbd/mainpage.htm
Rhode Island: http://www.health.state.ri.us
South Carolina: http://www.llr.state.sc.us/pol/nursing
South Dakota: http://www.state.sd.us/dcr/nursing/
Tennessee: http://170.142.76.180/bmf-bin/BMFproflist.pl
Texas RN: http://www.bne.state.tx.us/
Texas VN: http://www.bvne.state.tx.us/
Utah: http://www.commerce.state.ut.us/
Vermont: http://vtprofessionals.org/nurses/
Virginia: http://www.dhp.state.va.us/
Washington: http://www.doh.wa.gov/nursing/
West Virginia PN: http://www.lpnboard.state.wv.us/
West Virginia RN: http://www.state.wv.us/nurses/rn/
Wisconsin: http://www.drl.state.wi.us/
Wyoming: http://nursing.state.wy.us/

Appendix E
Example Strategy Forms
Strategy Form #1 "Title"

Used with permission from Chris Vaughan, RN. Nurses Brain. Portland, OR.

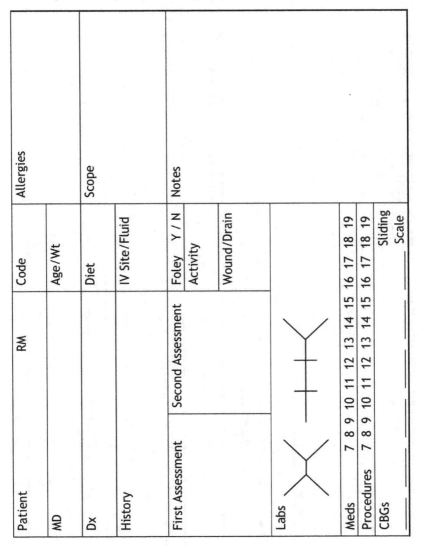

Suggested key:

\ = vital signs are charted   M = murmur
/ = assessment is charted   A = Plan of care charted

Strategy Form #2: Daily Update

Used with permission from Steve McAnally, RN.

Date

EC Assignment		

Patient Label
EM/PA/Res/NP

Shift Change Y/N	Bed Assignment/Time	Admission Information
To Bed From:		
Triage DG EMS	Report Called To/Time	Movement Time

DC Order Time	CC/MOI	Admit Dx	Allergies

Triage Chief Complaint	Triage ESI	IV Access	Past Medical/Surgical Hx	Vital Signs/Telemetry

Time Assessment Completed	Resources Used	Abnormal Labs	

Home Meds

	Yes	Foley	No	NG Tube	Yes	No	Other Tubes

Ht			Pending Labs/Procedures/Meds	

Wt	Flu	Pneum	Tet	Falls	Depress	Other	Plan

Time Medications Given

Rounding/Needs/Activity/MD Notification

Concerning Issues

Patient Label
EM/PA/Res/NP

Shift Change Y/N	Bed Assignment/Time	Admission Information
To Bed From:		
Triage DG EMS	Report Called To/Time	Movement Time

DC Order Time	CC/MOI	Admit Dx	Allergies

Triage Chief Complaint	Triage ESI	IV Access	Past Medical/Surgical Hx	Vital Signs/Telemetry

Time Assessment Completed	Resources Used	Abnormal Labs	

Home Meds

	Yes	Foley	No	NG Tube	Yes	No	Other Tubes

Ht			Pending Labs/Procedures/Meds	

Wt	Flu	Pneum	Tet	Falls	Depress	Other	Plan

Time Medications Given

Rounding/Needs/Activity/MD Notification

Concerning Issues

Strategy Form #3: Summary Report
by Rosale Lobo, RN, MSN, CNS, LNCC.

Name		Room	Admit	Date Age
Code Status/Allergies		Activity	FEN:	IV Access
S.0. #				Fluids
Diagnosis/Reason for Admission				
Chief MD:			Meds/Treatments	Assess/Intervene/ Respond (AIR)
Vital Signs			700	700
1st Set			800	800
2nd Set			900	900
3rd Set			1000	1000
Labs:			1100	1100
WBC:	BUN/Cr	GI	1200	1200
H/H:	Na	K Cl	1300	1300
Ph	Mg	Ca	1400	1400
PT/PTT/INR/aPTT			1500	1500
Cardiac:	NL	NN	1600	1600
Vascular:	NL	NN	1700	1700
Neuro:	NL	NN	1800	1800
GI Last BM:	NL	NN	1900	1900
GU:	NL	NN		
Resp:	NL	NN	Surgical	
Input/Output: Integument			Hx:	
Treatments: List			Headers:	
			Narrative Comments:	

231

Strategy Form #4: SBAR Report

Used with permission from Lorie Poulin RN

Privacy Code:
Team/Service:

Patient	LastSS#	Room	Date

Situation	Next of Kin:		Religion:

Background			Allergies:
			Isolation:
Code Status:	CPR ☐ Intubation ☐	Countershock ☐	Pressors ☐

Assessment	*Day* Nurse/NA	*Evening* Nurse/NA	*Night* Nurse/NA
Cognitive/ Behavioral Neuro Q4 ☐ QS ☐ Elopement Risk ☐ Secure Care ☐ CSM ☐ 1:1 ☐ Behavioral Flag ☐			
Restraints Date/Time went into restraint: Type: Initial note: Discontinue Note:	MD order every calendar day Bedside sheet complete: RN/NA	MD order every calendar day Bedside sheet complete: RN/NA	MD order every calendar day Bedside sheet complete: RN/NA
Vital Signs QS ☐ Q4 ☐ QS ☐			
Pain	Last pain med given: PRN Effectiveness within 1 hr ☐	Last pain med given: PRN Effectiveness within 1 hr ☐	Last pain med given: PRN Effectiveness within 1 hr ☐
Respiratory Incen Spirometer ☐ Lungs ☐			
Cardiovascular Venodynes ☐			
Gastrointestinal Last BM: FMS ☐			

Strategy Form #4: SBAR Report Continued.

Assessment	Day Nurse/NA	Evening Nurse/NA	Night Nurse/NA
Nutrition and Fluids 110 ☐ DailyWt ☐ Apiration Risk ☐			
Fingersticks Freq__ Coverage__	11a	5p 9p	7a
Drains			
GU Foley ☐ Texas/Condom ☐ Bladder Scan ☐ Frequency___			
IV/Access Type Saline Lock ☐ TLC ☐ PICC ☐ Hickman/Portcath ☐ Site Change Date: Tubing Change Date	Bag/Tubing labeled	Bag/Tubing labeled	Bag/Tubing labeled
Mobility/Fall Risk Last Morse Score: Green Armband ☐ Independent ☐ Partial Assist ☐ Complete Assist ☐	Activity:	Activity:	Activity:
Skin (Pressure Ulcer)	Skin reassess Braden 18 or < every 48 hours Skin reassess Braden >18-every Wednesday		
Last Braden Score:	7:30a-8p-rooms 42 through 11-4	7:30p-8a-rooms 13 through 21-4	
Specialty Mattress:			
Wound Consult:	Ulcer stage: Turn q2hr ☐	Ulcer stage: Turn q2hr ☐	Ulcer stage: Turn q2hr ☐
Next Reassessment:	Location:	Location:	Location:
Wound Care (Including surgical wounds, rashes, skin tears)			
Pertinent Labs/ Repletions	Blood transfusion forms completely filled and transfusion completed within 4 hrs of leaving blood bank		
Diagnostic Tests			

Continued on next page.

Strategy Form #4: SBAR Report Continued.

Assessment	*Day* Nurse/NA	*Evening* Nurse/NA	*Night* NurseiNA
D/C Plan Instructions □ Equipment □ Medications □ Travel □	□ MDorder □ PT Survey □ Lines DC'd □ Skin Note □ MRSA Swab □ DC Note □ Pneumovax □ Fluvax	□ MDorder □ PT Survey □ Lines DC'd □ Skin Note □ MRSA Swab □ DC Note □ Pneumovax □ Fluvax	□ MDorder □ PT Survey □ Lines DC'd □ Skin Note □ MRSA Swab □ DC Note □ Pneumovax □ Fluvax
Patient Education Needs	□ Completed □ Not Completed	□ Completed □ Not Completed	□ Completed □ Not Completed
Recommendation	*GOAL:*	*GOAL:*	*GOAL:*

Part 5:
The Side That Is Last, But Not Least

Contributions
by Nursing Professionals

LP's Story
15 years as a nurse
Surgery, PACU

I was working a temporary stint on nights in the PACU, helping them out because of a shortage. I usually work days.

Well, a week ago, I had a post-op neuro patient come in. I did a full assessment and wrote the findings on the SBAR, which is not part of our legal record. In our unit, there is no neuro assessment template on the electronic medical record. They have respiratory, cardiac, urinary, but no neuro. The patient was within normal limits on the assessment, but I didn't document it.

The next morning, the neurologist came in; the patient had deteriorated. There was no proof an assessment was done or that the patient had been stable. The doctor had no post-op baseline assessment to refer to in the electronic patient record. The SBAR is only a shift-to-shift hand off report for the nurses. Documenting in both places seems very repetitious, but in the end, nurses need to document in the patient's legal record, not just the shift report hand off tool.

KG's Story
35 years as a nurse
Medical Surgical, ER, Psych.

I was a clinical instructor for an LPN program. One of my students came to me to report an assessment finding – a deep purple (almost black) bruise from knee to groin in the inner right thigh and halfway around the leg.

We consulted the intake forms. The patient had been there two days; he was a right post-op hip replacement 7 days prior. This bruise was not mentioned in any of the previous documentation. The intake forms were "blank" under skin assessment; there were no nurses notes about it, and there were no labs (the patient was on Lovenox).

I reported these findings to the staff nurse but she would not call the MD. I reported these findings to the charge nurse. She would not call the MD. We documented findings and names of those reported to but.....still.....Wow!

CD's Story
14 years as a nurse
L&D

Electronic Charting – 20-year-old G1P0 admitted for primary C-section for breech presentation with a history of methadone use. The OR sponge count was correct x 2 per the OR circulating and scrub nurses. The MD also said the sponge count was correct. The patient presented with pain two weeks later and there was no intervention.

The patient presented to the MD's office 1 month later and an X-ray was done. The diagnosis was a retained sponge in her abdomen that was causing extensive bowel necrosis. It took her one year to recover with the support of a PICC for TPN and surgery.

The count was correct on the electronic charting.

She sued and was awarded a large monetary compensation.

WH's Story
Certified Life Care Planner

One of my favorites was a huge box where approximately one third of the pages were blank, except for a single word or number, e.g. "26.4" or "yes." No dates, signatures, legends, or clues. What do you suppose that 26.4 was? A hct, a bicarb, a mcg/kg.min? I have no idea.

I have seen pages of BP measurements so spread across the pages that it's impossible to follow or track to see what was happening to relate it to other facts. One of these came from records from a hospital chain where I have an old friend who is the director of nursing for all their hospitals; I sent a redacted copy to her and asked her if this is what her nurses have to work with, and if so, how do they know what they are doing?

Epilogue
The Final Side of the Story

If you fail to plan, you plan to fail. This might sound like a corny cliché, but it is really good advice. Strategic planning is a habit adopted by all successful professional businesses. Without a method of tracking your goals and progress towards them, how will you ever know if you are getting there? Knowledge of the healthcare laws plus a systemic approach can subtract you from the equation in a lawsuit. Be the nurse who has taken care of the patient and make plans to show that your documentation leaves nothing to the imagination.

Trust, but verify. Another corny phrase that packs a punch. As nurses, we share the responsibility to care for our patients with many members of the healthcare team. Some people we know; others, we've never seen before. As healthcare team members, we are all obligated to follow very similar standards of care. Being honest and ethical is understood. The sad part is that not everyone interprets honesty and ethics in the same way. You will be alone during deposition and on the witness stand, therefore your opinion of things must be regarded as firsthand knowledge. Double check the facts for yourself; once you do, you will sleep much better.

Know your electronic medical record. No cliché here, just the simple truth. Electronic medical records are everywhere. Some systems have become more popular within certain industries and some institutions have created ones for themselves. Regardless of their origins, it's better to know and understand all the indicators and categories of your software. The ultimate job of these programs is to assist in critical thinking and in the safe delivery of care. We are not there yet, so it is very important that you do not blindly trust the software to draw conclusions for you. Getting a strong handle on your software during the implementation stage is a perfect time to develop a documentation system that complements the software. Changes will continue to happen for many years to come; this is the perfect time to integrate your system of documentation with your facility's computer program.

You are a non-fiction storyteller. As a non-fiction writer, you are faced with the daily task of recreating the patient's assessment, your interventions, and their responses on a document, along with significant conversations. The idea of writing a first draft, then not reviewing it, is foreign to most writers, yet there are several studies that demonstrate that nurses are more effective communicators when we document in free-flowing paragraph form. Today, that writing style is less common, and it's soon to be non-existent. Remind yourself that, whenever possible, you should double-check your entries in order to verify for accuracy and content. Make whatever changes you need during this process that represent the message you are trying to send. Your double-check should tell you whether or not you're the effective communicator you think you are; only you can be the judge.

Be the Guinea Pig. It is not easy to have your work critiqued. The last thing you might want is to put yourself under the documentation microscope. But studies show that, when nurses are given instructions about their documentation within 24-48 hours after they have made entries, they are more likely to better understand the flow and expectations of the indicators in the software. Be willing to get critiqued; you'll have a better chance of getting things right sooner than later.

Patience is a virtue. Back to the clichés. Yes, having the patience to make changes in your professional patterns takes practice. It is expected as a professional nurse that you care for patients using all the safety measures available, that you make decisions based on your knowledge and experience and that your choices line up with those professionals in the same or similar venues. We are not given the tools to execute this mission in all the training that we receive, because the process of workflow comes on the job. Creating a strategic, systemic approach takes patience. Make changes slowly to your regimen and build on it regularly. Remember that, while patience is a virtue, having patients to care for is an honor.

Associate with professional organizations. If you do not belong to a professional organization, you might be surprised by the camaraderie that goes along with the membership. There is a sense of comfort when you surround yourself with people who understand your situation. With the Internet, it is not always necessary to show up in person; virtual companionship can begin the dialogue necessary to keep current with standards. Groups provide avenues to find the information that keeps your knowledge base validated. In nursing, we need each other more than we realize.

Utilize personal software shortcuts. The standards of care are found on government sites and through professional journals and organizations. There are a host of companies that make up-to-date healthcare information available for you to place on your personal device. These products provide up-to-date information on standards. When looking for information to help educate yourself and your patients, look for shortcuts. Time is precious; take the time to download software that will allow your assessments and documentation to shine. Ask the doctors you work with; many of them carry volumes of information on a personal handheld device, and you should, too.

Use the strategic planning process in other areas of your life. Planning a strategy sheet is a great way to get a handle on your nursing shift. Having a mission statement, understanding mandates, and creating a system that envisions an outcome are useful in all areas of life. Plan on staying out of court, but also plan on making a professional impression that keeps you excited about nursing. Use the steps provided to organize and move forward in healthcare. Collectively, nurses are a powerful group. Decide to contribute to that force with a plan of action.

Keep your focus on the end-game. There are so many reasons not to put the systems in place to keep yourself accountable. But there are more reasons to make certain that you hold yourself accountable before anyone else challenges your skills. There is something very stressful about a lawyer who questions your ability to adequately care for patients.

How can the attorney ask questions about the care you've provided when they do not possess the knowledge and skills to care for unhealthy people? Because they study the standards of practice and all the research available. Do not allow yourself to become a defendant. Outsmart the lawyers and put a plan in place now, as that's the best way to win.

About the Author

Rosale Lobo, RN, MSN, CNS, LNCC

Rosale has always had a passion for nursing. She began in Brooklyn, NY earning a BSN from Long Island University. Rosale was eager to nurse and excited about the many roles a nurse can have. She completed her Masters degree from Hunter College (NY) in 1989. Rosale took several positions in management, but felt most comfortable at the bedside. She was never afraid to float, work as an agency nurse or travel nurse. This gypsy like pattern created a clinical nursing experience that was very diverse. It forced her to develop documentation strategies that kept her free from scrutiny. Rosale realized that when a new situation arose, the facility would orient her to the paperwork, not to the documentation.

In 2003, Rosale became a legal nurse consultant. She has the pleasure of working with prominent plaintiff medical malpractice attorneys in many states. This experience deepened her desire to speak to nurses about documentation. Nurses need to protect themselves from lawyers who have no regard for healthcare working conditions. Patient acuity is on the rise and the number of co-morbidities you have to manage has become intense. Having a documentation system is crucial to license protection. The electronic medical record is not the answer. A personal system of accountability is.

Rosale is enrolled in Walden University pursuing a doctorate degree in Public Policy Administration: Healthcare. Her intention is to create documentation education awareness for nurses. She believes healthcare facilities should provide documentation classes for nurses. She's convinced this will decrease litigation and reimbursement denials, and increase more effective hand off communication.

www.loboconsulting.com